BASEBALL'S
GREATEST
ALL-STAR GAMES

BASEBALL'S GREATEST ALL-STAR GAMES

Howard Liss

David McKay Company, Inc.
New York

*For my brother, Eddie, who taught me
how to play and appreciate baseball.
And for Steve, Sheri, Benjie, and
Alex, who staged such a comeback.*

Library of Congress Cataloging in Publication Data

Liss, Howard.
  Baseball's greatest all-star games.

  Includes index.
  SUMMARY: Describes 10 outstanding All Star
Games from 1934 to 1977.
  1. All-Star Baseball Game—History—Juvenile
literature. [1. All-Star Baseball Game—History.
2. Baseball—History] I. Title.
GV875.A1L57   796.357'784   79-2152

ISBN 0-679-20527-6

1 2   3   4   5   6   7   8   9   10

Manufactured in the United States of America

CONTENTS

Introduction

It all began in 1933. America was bogged down in the Great Depression. Baseball attendance was slipping. The game needed a boost.

Arch Ward, the great *Chicago Tribune* sportswriter, dreamed up an idea for a special game, to be played in mid-season, between the greatest stars of the National and American Leagues. Ward reasoned that the fans would benefit because they would have an opportunity to watch almost all of baseball's superstars in a single game. Baseball would benefit because the old argument would start again: Which is stronger—the National or the American League? The United Charities, Catholic Charities, and Jewish Charities in and around Chicago would benefit from the proceeds. Besides, Chicago was holding a world's fair in 1933, called the "Century of Progress International Exposition." Fans who came to the city to view the fair were bound to attend the game.

Arch Ward was right. The first game was played before 49,000 fans in Comiskey Park, the home of the Chicago White Sox. And the fans saw a very good game. Two home runs were hit, one by Frankie Frisch, the St. Louis Cardinals' second baseman. The other was hit by Babe Ruth, and it proved to be the margin of victory, as the American League defeated the National League 4–2.

The loudest cheers were reserved for Carl Hubbell, the ace left-hander of the New York Giants. As he was warming up to enter the game as a relief pitcher, the fans gave him an ovation. Obviously, they had read newspaper accounts of the game Hubbell had pitched only the previous Sunday. He had faced the tough St. Louis Cardinals and pitched an 18-inning shutout! Hubbell had given up only six hits, four of them infield dribblers. His pitching opponent, Tex Carleton, had gone 16 scoreless innings before calling it a day.

The first all-star game was so successful that the officials of both leagues agreed to make it an annual event. Only in one year, 1945, was the game cancelled, because of wartime travel restrictions. Every major league city would take turns playing host. The all-star game became so popular that, for a period of years, two games were played annually, but that proved too difficult due to the 162-game schedule.

Through the years there have been exciting all-star games and dull games. There have been pitchers' battles, slugfests, and one-sided games. The low-scoring games have been left out because they tend to be dull when described in a book. Perhaps some fans who are familiar with the all-star series may disagree with the games chosen to be recreated. That's all right, too. To call these "the greatest all-star games" is merely one person's opinion. Good arguments are part of baseball.

Probably many young readers will not recognize some of the names listed in the box scores. The author can only advise the study of a good baseball record book. Then such names as Lou Gehrig, Pie Traynor, Jimmy Foxx, Bill Terry, Heinie Manush, Charlie Gehringer, and a hundred others will take on new meaning.

July 10, 1934—
The Polo Grounds,
New York

In 1934, baseball's Hall of Fame had not yet been established. However, the names of *all* the starting batsmen in the American League lineup would some day be entered in baseball's shrine at Cooperstown, New York. The infield consisted of the Yankees' Lou Gehrig at first base; Charlie Gehringer of the Tigers at second; Joe Cronin, the Washington player-manager, at shortstop; and Jimmy "Double-X" Foxx of Philadelphia at third. In the outfield were Heinie Manush of Washington, Al Simmons of the White Sox, and Babe Ruth, the all-time Yankee slugger. Behind the plate was another Yankee, Bill Dickey.

The National League roster was also liberally sprinkled with future Hall of Famers, such as Bill Terry, Joe "Ducky" Medwick, Carl Hubbell, Frankie Frisch, and Pie Traynor.

Baseball officials had agreed that the teams would be managed by the skippers who had won pennants in their respective leagues the previous year. Therefore, Joe Cronin, whose Washington Senators had finished first in the American League in 1933, piloted the American

Joe Medwick, of the St. Louis Cardinals, crosses the home plate after his homer in the third inning of the all-star game on July 10, 1934.

League squad. The Giants, who had won in the National League (and the World Series as well) should have been managed by John McGraw. But he had passed away shortly before spring training. The Giants' new manager was Bill Terry, their first baseman. He automatically became the field boss of the National League team.

In one other respect the 1934 game was sad. It would be Babe Ruth's last all-star appearance wearing a Yankee uniform. Babe had announced that it would be his final season as a regular ball player. He was forty years old, and his batting eye was dimmed. True, he could still drive the ball out of the park. Only a few days earlier, Babe had slugged the 699th home run of his fabulous career. But he was overweight, and he found it difficult to go nine innings. In 1934 he would hit only 22 homers—practically a batting slump for the Babe.

With or without Ruth, the American League lineup was a terrifying sight for any pitcher. Leading off was second baseman Charlie Gehringer of Detroit. Charlie was hitting .381. In second spot was Heinie Manush of the Washington Senators, leading the league with .403. Third was Babe Ruth, who, even near the end of his career, had hit 13 home runs at the all-star break. Batting cleanup was first baseman Lou Gehrig, hitting .367 with 24 home runs. In the fifth slot was Jimmy Foxx (who had already belted 26 home runs), followed by Al Simmons who had 13 home runs to his credit so far.

The National League batters weren't exactly weaklings either. Bill Terry was hitting .367; Kiki Cuyler, the Chicago Cubs' brilliant outfielder, was at .352; and hard-hitting Joe Medwick was hitting .349 with 10 home runs.

But the player everyone had really come to see was the Giants' ace left-hander, Carl Hubbell. Fifty thousand fans journeyed to the Polo Grounds to watch the pitcher who had led the Giants to a pennant and victory in the World Series. New York sportswriters had nicknamed Carl Hubbell "The Meal Ticket." Whenever the Giants needed a victory badly, Hubbell delivered it.

Hubbell's best pitch was a screwball, which is a reverse curve. Normally, when a lefty pitcher faces a right-handed batter, the curve ball will break to the inside of the plate. Hubbell's screwball broke down and away from a right-handed batter. When facing a left-handed hitter, Hubbell used a normal curve, which also broke away.

However, the ball probably did not break enough when Gehringer led off, because the second baseman banged a single to center and took second when Wally Berger fumbled the ball momentarily. Heinie Manush drew a pass. With two men on and nobody out, Hubbell had to face Babe Ruth, Lou Gehrig, and Jimmy Foxx. Those three had already accounted for 63 home runs in regular season play.

The infield clustered around Hubbell for a quick conference. "Are you okay, Hub?" asked a worried Bill Terry.

"Sure I am," Hubbell said quietly. "Get back to your positions and let me pitch."

Babe Ruth stepped up to the plate. Hubbell struck him out with four pitches.

Lou Gehrig, another left-handed batter, dug in. Hubbell struck him out.

Up came Jimmy Foxx, a righty hitter. Hubbell struck him out.

It was unbelievable! With thirteen pitches, Carl Hubbell had fanned three of the greatest batters in baseball history. Only Foxx had managed to tick the ball for a foul.

Frankie Frisch hit a home run off Lefty Gomez, the Yankee pitcher starting for the American League. The Nationals were leading 1–0 as the second inning got under way. But the fans were still buzzing about Hubbell. Al Simmons stepped into the batter's box, waving his bat menacingly as he eyed the ace left-hander. Hubbell struck him out. Joe Cronin took his stance. Hubbell struck him out.

Bill Dickey, the Yankee catcher, broke the spell by lacing out a single. He was followed by Lefty Gomez, one of the weakest batters in baseball. Hubbell slipped over a strike. Gomez swung at the next offering, missed it, and the bat slipped out of his hands. It bounced all the way out near second base.

"Leave it there," growled Frankie Frisch, as the bat boy ran out to retrieve it. "He won't need it anyhow."

4

Gomez struck out.

In the third inning, the National League increased its lead to 4–0. Frisch walked, Pie Traynor singled, and Joe Medwick stroked one into the upper left field stands.

Lon Warneke, the Chicago Cubs' great pitcher, took over for Hubbell in the fourth inning, since starting pitchers usually went no more than three innings. He was roughed up almost immediately. Al Simmons, who had fanned in the second inning, lined a shot that bounced off the wall on the fly for a two-base hit. Joe Cronin singled scoring Simmons. One out later, Earl Averill, a slugging Cleveland outfielder, pinch hit for Gomez and crashed a triple off the bleacher wall in right-center, scoring Cronin. That made the score 4–2, in favor of the Nationals.

The American League continued the barrage of base hits in the fifth inning. Ruth and Gehrig walked. Foxx hit to center off relief pitcher Van Lingle Mungo of the Dodgers to score one run. Simmons legged out a grounder to short for another hit, scoring Gehrig and making it a 4–4 tie. Mungo got Cronin to foul out, but Bill Dickey walked to load the bases. Averill, who had remained in the game after his triple, banged a two-bagger down the right field foul line to score another pair of runs. An intentional walk to Gehringer loaded the bases again.

Because of the various substitutions, the next batter was Red Ruffing, a Yankee right-handed pitcher. Red was one of the best hitting-pitchers in all of baseball, and he proved it with a line single for two more runs. The score was 8–4 by the time the American League was finally retired, after scoring six big runs.

Ben Chapman, another Yankee outfielder, replaced Babe Ruth in right field. It turned out to be a shrewd defensive move. The Nationals came roaring back, and only a fine play by Chapman helped stop the rally.

"Pepper" Martin, the speedy Cardinal third baseman, drew a pass to start the surge. Frisch, Pie Traynor, and pinch hitter Chuck Klein singled for two runs. Mel Ott, the superb Giants' outfielder and future Hall of Fame player, batted for Kiki Cuyler and sent a liner toward right. Chapman tore in but couldn't quite make the catch. However, Klein had to hold up between first and second because he wasn't sure the ball would drop in. When it fell, Klein tried for second, but it was too late. Chapman grabbed the ball and fired it to second base for the force-out. Had the old,

Pepper Martin, Cardinal infielder, arrives safely at third on Frisch's single in the fifth inning of the 1934 all-star game.

BOX SCORES

AMERICAN

	ab	r	h	rbi
Gehringer, Det. 2b	3	0	2	0
Manush, Wash. lf	2	0	0	0
Ruffing, NY p	1	0	1	2
Harder, Cleve. p	2	0	0	0
Ruth, NY rf	2	1	0	0
Chapman, NY rf	2	0	1	0
Gehrig, NY 1b	4	1	0	0
Foxx, Phila. 3b	5	1	2	1
Simmons, Chi. cf-lf	5	3	3	1
Cronin, Wash. ss	5	1	2	2
Dickey, NY c	2	1	1	0
Cochrane, Det. c	1	0	0	0
Gomez, NY p	1	0	0	0
Averill, Cleve. cf	4	1	2	3
West, St. L. cf	0	0	0	0
	39	9	14	9

NATIONAL

	ab	r	h	rbi
Frisch, St. L. 2b	3	3	2	1
Herman, Chi. 2b	2	0	1	0
Traynor, Pitt. 3b	5	2	2	1
Medwick, St. L. lf	2	1	1	3
Klein, Chi. lf	3	0	1	1
Cuyler, Chi. rf	2	0	0	0
Ott, NY rf	2	0	0	0
Berger, Bost. cf	2	0	0	0
P. Waner, Pitt. cf	2	0	0	0
Terry, NY 1b	3	0	1	0
Jackson, NY ss	2	0	0	0
Vaughan, Pitt. ss	2	0	0	0
Hartnett, Chi. c	2	0	0	0
Lopez, B'klyn. c	2	0	0	0
Hubbell, NY p	0	0	0	0
Warneke, Chi. p	0	0	0	0
Martin, St. L.	1	1	0	0
Frankhouse, Bost. p	1	0	0	0
	36	7	8	6

LINE SCORE

		R	H	E
American	000 261 000 =	9	14	1
National	103 030 000 =	7	8	1

Errors: Berger, Gehrig. Left on base: American 12, National 5. Double plays (1). Two-base hits: Foxx, Simmons (2), Cronin, Averill, Herman. Three-base hits: Chapman, Averill. Home runs: Frisch, Medwick. Hits: off Gomez 3 in 3 innings; off Ruffing 4 in 1 (none out in fifth); off Harder, 1 in 5; off Hubbell 2 in 3; off Warneke 3 in 1 (none out in fifth); off Mungo 4 in 1; off Dean 5 in 3; off Frankhouse 0 in 1. Struck out: by Hubbell 6; by Gomez 3; by Harder 2; by Warneke 1; by Mungo 1; by Dean 4. Bases on balls: off Gomez 1; off Ruffing 1; off Harder 1; off Hubbell 2; off Warneke 3; off Mungo 2; off Dean 1; off Frankhouse 1. Winning pitcher—Harder. Losing Pitcher—Mungo. Umpires: Pfirman, Owens, Stark and Moriarty.

slower Babe Ruth been in right field, the play could not have been made.

Paul "Big Poison" Waner batted for Wally Berger and struck out. But on the third strike, the Nationals pulled a double steal with Traynor racing home for the third run of the inning.

The American League got one run back on doubles by Simmons and Cronin to make the score 9–7.

And that was how the game ended. The American League couldn't add any more runs, but neither could the National League.

There were a few peculiar incidents in the game. Billy Herman, a substitute infielder, came in as a pinch hitter in the third inning and was retired. He went back to the dugout and sat on the bench when the National League took the field. That meant he could not get back in the game. Yet, in the seventh inning, he played second base. Nobody said anything. Perhaps nobody noticed. In the sixth inning, Joe Cronin was at second base and Mickey Cochrane on first with one out. Both were player-managers. Earl Averill came to bat and struck out. Cronin and Cochrane had taken long leads off their bases, and catcher Al Lopez knew they couldn't get back in time. Holding the ball, Lopez ran all the way out to the shortstop position. He missed the tag on Cronin but threw to Arky Vaughan, who tagged him out. Just for fun, Lopez then tagged out Cochrane to make it four outs in the inning. Then he remarked: "Hey, player-managers, what would you have done if a couple of your players pulled a rock like that?"

Regardless of the final outcome, the 1934 game will always stand out as the one in which a great pitcher struck out five of baseball's greatest hitters in succession.

July 8, 1941—
Briggs Stadium,
Detroit

It was the year of Joe DiMaggio's record-breaking hitting streak. On the Sunday before the all-star game, big Joe had six hits in a doubleheader. He had hit safely in forty-eight consecutive games (it would run to fifty-six before he was finally stopped). DiMaggio was batting .357.

That year, Ted Williams would hit .406. He was hitting over .400 at the all-star break.

DiMaggio and Williams were often discussed by baseball fans, managers, and other players. Both were considered the top outfielders in the American League. Perhaps Williams was a slightly superior batter, but DiMaggio was the better fielder. However, everyone thought that each would be even greater if they switched teams, with DiMaggio going to Boston and Williams coming to New York. Both were certain to add twenty points to their batting averages and probably a dozen more home runs. Of course, Yankee and Red Sox fans would have been enraged if such a trade took place, but it really did make sense.

DiMaggio was a right-handed hitter, Williams batted

Ted Williams, left, of the Boston Red Sox, who blasted a ninth-inning homer that defeated the National League all-stars, rejoices in the locker room with Joe DiMaggio, American League teammate and New York Yankee star.

lefty. But both could hit right-handed pitchers and southpaws equally well. The trouble lay in their home parks.

DiMaggio's "power alley"—the area his batted balls often reached—was left center. The fence in that section was over 450 feet from the plate. DiMaggio would belt 400-foot fly balls, which would have been home runs in Boston's Fenway Park, but in Yankee Stadium, they were merely long outs.

Williams's problem was like DiMag's, only in reverse. His booming drives went to right or right-center, but the right center bleachers were more than 400 feet away. In Yankee Stadium, they would have been home runs, but in Fenway Park, the fielders could catch the ball.

DiMaggio and Williams were only two of the reasons the American League was favored to win the ball game. Starting for the team was Bob Feller, whose fast ball looked like a tiny white pill as it zoomed to the plate. Measuring instruments had not really been perfected in

1941, but by using various devices, someone managed to time Feller's fast ball at 100 miles an hour. Feller also had a slider that broke sharply just before it reached the plate. The average batter seldom got a hit off Feller, who had already won sixteen games and lost only four.

Feller showed his stuff to the National League batsmen for three innings. Only Lonny Frey, the Cincinnati second baseman, was bold enough to reach Feller for a base hit. Feller promptly picked him off first. During his turn on the mound, the Cleveland right-hander fanned four.

The American League hitters were equally helpless against starting pitcher Whitlow Wyatt, the idol of Brooklyn Dodger fans. Wyatt, the winner of thirteen games so far, also had a good fast ball, a sharp curve, and a nice changeup that kept the batters off stride. He pitched two innings and faced the minimum of six men. Only Ted Williams got on by a walk, but Jeff Heath grounded into a double play.

Ted Williams is greeted at home plate by teammate Joe DiMaggio, left, and coach Marv Shea, after Williams hit a ninth-inning home run to give the American League a 7–5 victory over the National League in the 1941 all-star game.

The first six innings were merely routine. The American League broke the ice in the fourth on doubles by Cecil Travis and Ted Williams to go ahead, 1–0. The Nationals tied it in the top of the sixth on a two-base hit by pitcher Bucky Walters. He scored when Heath muffed Pete Reiser's high fly. The American Leaguers regained the lead in the bottom half on a couple of walks and an error by Reiser. At this point, it was just another ball game to the fans at Briggs Stadium.

Sid Hudson, of Washington, was on the mound when Enos Slaughter got a hit and went to second on Williams's error. Up stepped Arky Vaughan, the Pittsburgh shortstop. Vaughan had one of the most peculiar stances in baseball. A left-handed batter, Vaughan was almost facing the pitcher. He claimed he could see the ball better when he didn't have to turn his neck so much. He proved that the stance was perfect for him. Hudson fired a fast ball, and Vaughan creamed it into the upper deck for a two-run homer. That made the score 3–2 in favor of the Nationals.

The score suddenly became 5–2 in the top of the eighth. Johnny Mize doubled, and Vaughan came to the plate again. Once more, he put the wood to a fast ball. His second home run of the game did not travel quite as far, only reaching the second deck of the right field stands.

Joe DiMaggio's bat had been strangely silent all through the game. The American League got one run back through the efforts of DiMaggio and his brother, Dom, who played center field for the Boston Red Sox. Joe slammed a double into left center, and after Williams struck out, little brother Dom delivered Joe with a sharp single up the middle. Grinning, Dom later said, "I think Joe wouldn't have talked to me if I didn't get him home."

BOX SCORES

AMERICAN

	ab	r	h	rbi
Doerr, Bost. 2b	3	0	0	0
Gordon, NY 2b	2	1	1	0
Travis, Wash. 3b	4	1	1	0
J. DiMaggio, NY cf	4	3	1	1
Williams, Bost. lf	4	1	2	4
Heath, Cleve. rf	2	0	0	0
D. DiMaggio, Bost. rf	1	0	1	1
Cronin, Bost. ss	2	0	0	0
Boudreau, Cleve. ss	2	0	2	1
York, Det. 1b	3	0	1	0
Foxx, Bost. 1b	1	0	0	0
Dickey, NY c	3	0	1	0
Hayes, Phila. c	1	0	0	0
Cullenbine, St. L.	1	0	0	0
Feller, Cleve. p	0	0	0	0
Lee, Chi. p	1	0	0	0
Hudson, Wash. p	0	0	0	0
Keller, NY	1	0	0	0
Smith, Chi. p	0	0	0	0
Keltner, Cleve.	1	1	1	0
	36	7	11	7

NATIONAL

	ab	r	h	rbi
Hack, Chi. 3b	2	0	1	0
Lavagetto, B'klyn. 3b	1	0	0	0
Moore, St. L. lf	3	0	0	1
Reiser, B'klyn. cf	4	0	0	0
Mize, St. L. 1b	4	1	1	0
McCormick, Cin. 1b	0	0	0	0
Nicholson, Chi. rf	1	0	0	0
Elliott, Pitt. rf	1	0	0	0
Slaughter, St. L. rf	2	1	1	0
Vaughan, Pitt. ss	4	2	3	4
Miller, Bost. ss	0	0	0	0
Frey, Cin. 2b	1	0	1	0
Herman, B'klyn. 2b	3	0	2	0
Owen, B'klyn. c	1	0	0	0
Lopez, Pitt. c	1	0	0	0
Danning, NY c	1	0	0	0
Wyatt, B'klyn. p	0	0	0	0
Ott, NY	1	0	0	0
Derringer, Cin. p	0	0	0	0
Walters, Cin. p	1	1	1	0
Medwick, B'klyn.	1	0	0	0
Passeau, Chi. p	1	0	0	0
	33	5	10	5

LINE SCORE

				R	H	E
National	000	001	220	= 5	10	2
American	000	101	014	= 7	11	3

Errors: Heath, Reiser (2), Williams, Smith. Left on base: National 6, American 7. Double plays (2). Two-base hits: Mize, Slaughter, Herman, Walters, Travis, J. DiMaggio, Williams. Home runs: Vaughan (2), Williams. Hits: off Feller 1 in 3 innings; off Lee 4 in 3; off Hudson 3 in 1; off Smith 2 in 3; off Wyatt 0 in 2; off Derringer 2 in 2; off Walters 3 in 2; off Passeau 6 in 2 2/3. Bases on balls: off Wyatt 1; off Walters 2; off Hudson 1; off Passeau 1. Struck out: by Feller 4; by Derringer 1; by Walters 2; by Hudson 1; by Smith 2; by Passeau 3. Winning pitcher—Smith. Losing pitcher—Passeau. Umpires: Summers, Jorda, Grieve and Pinelli.

Claude Passeau, of the Cubs, was pitching when the game went into the bottom of the ninth. He retired the first batter, and it looked like the game was over. But nobody started for the aisles. With so many great hitters in the American League lineup, one quick burst of hits could change things around. Sure enough, pinch hitters Kenny Keltner and Joe Gordon rapped out singles. Cecil Travis walked to load the bases. Then Joe DiMaggio came to bat. It was the perfect time for the Yankee Clipper to become a hero with a slash of his bat. Instead, DiMaggio almost became the goat. He sent a hard bouncer to Eddie Miller at short. Miller flipped to Billy Herman for the force. It was a sure double play—except that Herman, in his eagerness, threw high and wide to first. DiMag beat the DP as a run scored to make it a 5–4 game.

Ted Williams stepped in. A hit would tie the score; an extra base hit might win it. Perhaps Passeau was unsettled because he had lost the double play. Or, maybe he just wanted to challenge the mighty Williams. He threw his best fast ball. Williams took his cut, and the ball went high and far against the roof of Briggs Stadium for a three-run homer and a 7–5 victory for the American League.

Cincinnati's Bill McKechnie, who had managed the National League, was asked why he didn't bring in a new pitcher to face Williams. McKechnie was accustomed to the second guessers in sports. Patiently, he explained that Passeau was an outstanding pitcher. He had almost gotten out of the inning on DiMaggio's grounder, which should have been turned into a double play. "With a lineup like the American League had, you just can't give them four outs and get away with it," McKechnie said.

July 9, 1946—
Fenway Park,
Boston

The all-star games played during World War II were really not worthy of the all-star name. Nearly all the great young players were in the service: Ted Williams, Joe DiMaggio, Bob Feller, Stan Musial, and scores of others. But now they were back, better than ever. Managers Steve O'Neill of Detroit and "Jolly Cholly" Grimm of Chicago put together their best players. However, one look at the American League roster showed clearly that the National League didn't have a chance.

Leading the pitching staff, as usual, was "Rapid Robert" Feller, the fireball king of the major leagues. Feller had already won fifteen games, including six shutouts. One of them was a no-hitter against the Yankees. It was the second no-hitter of Feller's career, since he had slammed the door against Chicago on opening day, 1940. In 1951, he would victimize Detroit with his third no-hit game.

Hal Newhouser, the Detroit Tigers' ace, looked even better, having won sixteen games so far. Other strong pitchers included Dave "Boo" Ferriss of Boston, Mickey

15

Harris, Jack Kramer, and Spud Chandler. Steve O'Neill said he didn't think too many of his pitchers would see action.

Joe DiMaggio would not get into the game because he had hurt his leg when sliding a few days previously. But that was no consolation to the National League. His place in center field was taken by Joe's brother, Dom, who was rolling merrily through opposing pitchers at a .349 clip. Not to be overlooked was Charlie "King Kong" Keller of the Yanks. Keller was built like a gorilla, with a hairy chest and powerful arms. When he hit the ball squarely, it went into orbit. He was batting .329, and had eighteen homers. And, of course, the big man in the batting order was "The Splendid Splinter," Theodore Samuel Williams.

It was really impossible to pitch to Ted Williams. He had developed batting to a science. He didn't look like a

Ted Williams, the slugging outfielder of the Boston Red Sox, after connecting with Rip Sewell's pitch. Williams's two home runs in the 1946 all-star game paced the American Leaguers to an easy win.

powerful man, yet with one flick of the bat, he made the ball jump into the bleachers. "The secret is in my wrists," Williams often explained. He would hold small rubber balls in each hand and squeeze them continuously. This simple exercise developed his wrists and forearms.

Williams was the last major leaguer to hit .400. In 1941, he batted .406, with 37 home runs and 120 runs batted in. Yet he didn't win the Most Valuable Player honor; the award was given to Joe DiMaggio. The following year, Williams "slipped" down to a .356 average. Then he joined the Marines and became a flying instructor. Now, in 1946, he was back at his old tricks, batting .347 with 23 home runs.

The National League pitching staff boasted no one with an outstanding record. None had won more than eight games. But one of the more interesting hurlers was Truett "Rip" Sewell of the Pittsburgh Pirates. In 1941, Sewell had an accident while deer hunting. A fellow hunter fired his shotgun and the pellets hit Sewell's right foot. He recovered but found that he would have to change his pitching motion. While experimenting with various grips, Sewell learned how to throw a kind of "blooper" pitch. He gripped the ball's seam with three fingers and lofted it toward the plate. The pitch moved slowly, about fifteen feet up in the air, but it had a lot of backspin. As the ball came down over the plate, no one could hit it solidly. It was difficult to judge the ball's height, as it drifted lazily downward, and most batters would swing too hard. One of Sewell's teammates named that pitch "the eephus ball."

Before the game started, Williams asked Sewell, "Hey, Rip, if you get into the game today, are you going to use the eephus ball?"

"Sure," Sewell grinned, "and I'll throw it to you, too."

But Williams didn't get a good ball to hit in his first time at bat, drawing a walk. A moment later, King Kong Keller blasted one into the right field seats, giving the Americans a 2–0 lead.

The Dodgers' Kirby Higbe was pitching when Williams dug in at the plate in the fourth inning. Higbe fired his best fast ball. Williams swung smoothly. The ball went into the right field stands like a homing pigeon looking for its roost.

By the fifth inning, it seemed that the American League was simply taking batting practice instead of playing an all-star game. A couple of hits and a walk filled the bases. Vern Stephens doubled-in a pair of runs, and Williams's base hit accounted for another. The lead was 6–0. By the end of the seventh, it was 8–0. Williams got his third hit, an infield single. King Kong walked, and Joe "Flash" Gordon delivered them both with a ringing two-bagger.

Meanwhile, the forces of the National League were marching up to the plate, taking their swings, and usually trailing dejectedly back to the dugout. Bob Feller allowed two hits in three innings and called it a day. Hal Newhouser grudgingly let the Nationals have one base hit in his turn on the mound. Jack Kramer, who followed Newhouser, didn't allow any hits at all.

It was not until the eighth inning that Ted Williams confronted Rip Sewell. By then, the game was almost over. The Americans had scored another run and had two men on base. The two men smiled at each other. Sewell went into his stretch and threw the eephus ball. Up and up it went, then it began to float downward across the plate.

Williams waited on the pitch. He swung hard. All he could do was tick a little foul.

Sewell was laughing now. Once more he threw that high rainbow pitch. Williams let it go for ball one. Then Sewell surprised Williams by slipping a fast ball in for strike two. Williams backed away from the plate and picked up a handful of dirt. So, it was to be a guessing game, was it? But Williams knew that Sewell would try the eephus pitch again. Why not? The game was lost, what was wrong with having a little fun? Williams would look mighty silly striking out on a big blooper pitch.

Sewell stretched and delivered. Williams was ready. He timed the pitch perfectly, taking a couple of steps forward. Then Williams brought his bat around in that sweet, level swing. When his bat met the ball, the right fielder hardly moved from his tracks. He just watched as the ball buzzed in a high arc into the right field stands for Williams's second home run of the ball game.

The final score was 12–0, but that wasn't very impor-

Ted Williams, left, and Charlie Keller of the New York Yankees, in the dressing room at Fenway Park, after the 1946 all-star game.

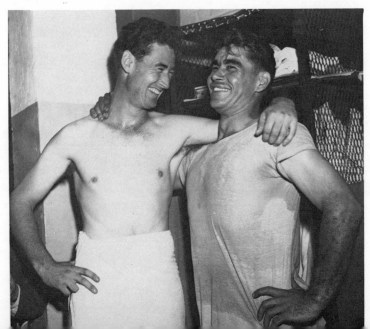

tant. The 1946 all-star game could be described as "The Ted Williams Show." In five trips to the plate, he had walked once, and hit two singles and two home runs. He had also batted in five runs—an all-star record at that time.

Best of all, in Williams's eyes, was the fact that he was the only batter ever to hit a home run off Rip Sewell's eephus pitch.

BOX SCORES

AMERICAN	ab	r	h	rbi	NATIONAL	ab	r	h	rbi
D. DiMaggio, Bost. cf	2	0	1	0	Schoendienst, St. L. 2b	2	0	0	0
Spence, Wash. cf	0	1	0	0	Gustine, Pitt. 2b	1	0	0	0
Chapman, Phila. cf	2	0	0	1	Musial, St. L. lf	2	0	0	0
Pesky, Bost. ss	2	0	0	0	Ennis, Phila. lf	2	0	0	0
Stephens, St. L. ss	3	1	2	2	Hopp, Bost. cf	2	0	1	0
Williams, Bost. lf	4	4	4	5	Lowrey, Chi. cf	2	0	1	0
Keller, NY rf	4	2	1	2	Walker, B'klyn. rf	3	0	0	0
Doerr, Bost. 2b	2	0	0	0	Slaughter, St. L. rf	1	0	0	0
Gordon, NY 2b	2	0	1	2	Kurowski, St. L. 3b	3	0	0	0
Vernon, Wash. 1b	2	0	0	0	Verban, Phila.	1	0	0	0
York, Bost. 1b	2	0	1	0	Mize, NY 1b	1	0	0	0
Keltner, Cleve. 3b	0	0	0	0	McCormick, Phila. 1b	1	0	0	0
Stirnweiss, NY 3b	3	1	1	0	Cavaretta, Chi. 1b	1	0	0	0
Hayes, Cleve. c	1	0	0	0	W. Cooper, NY c	1	0	1	0
Rosar, Phila. c	2	1	1	0	Masi, Bost. c	2	0	0	0
Wagner, Bost. c	1	0	0	0	Marion, St. L. ss	3	0	0	0
Feller, Cleve. p	0	0	0	0	Passeau, Chi. p	1	0	0	0
Appling, Chi.	1	0	0	0	Higbe, B'klyn. p	1	0	0	0
Newhouser, Det. p	1	1	1	0	Blackwell, Cin. p	0	0	0	0
Dickey, NY	1	0	0	0	Lamanno, Cin.	1	0	0	0
Kramer, St. L. p	1	1	1	0	Sewell, Pitt. p	0	0	0	0
	36	12	14	12		31	0	3	0

LINE SCORE				R	H	E
National	000	000	000	= 0	3	0
American	200	130	24x	= 12	14	1

Error: Pesky. Two-base hits: Stephens, Gordon. Home runs: Keller, Williams (2). Double plays: (2). Left on base: National 5; American 4. Hits: off Feller 2 in 3 innings; off Newhouser 1 in 3; off Kramer 0 in 3; off Passeau 2 in 3; off Higbe 5 in 1 1/3; off Blackwell 3 in 2 2/3; off Sewell 4 in 1. Bases on balls: off Passeau 2; off Higbe 1; off Blackwell 1; off Kramer 1. Struck out: by Feller 3; by Newhouser 4; by Higbe 2; by Blackwell 1; by Kramer 3. Wild pitch: Blackwell. Winning pitcher—Feller. Losing pitcher—Passeau. Umpires: Summers, Boggess, Rommel, Goetz.

July 12, 1949—
Ebbets Field,
Brooklyn

For the first time in baseball's history, there were black players on the field in an all-star game. Three of them played for the Brooklyn Dodgers: Jackie Robinson, Roy Campanella, and Don Newcombe. The fourth was Larry Doby, the hard-hitting outfielder who played for the Cleveland Indians. But it had been Robinson who broke the color line and became the first black player in the major leagues.

Robinson had been a star athlete in high school and college, winning letters in several sports. He was discovered by Branch Rickey, general manager of the Dodgers, while playing for the Kansas City Monarchs, an all-black team. Rickey signed up Robinson and sent him to the Montreal Royals, a Dodger farm team. On opening day, against the Jersey City Giants, Robbie had two singles and a home run and stole two bases. He went on to win the batting championship of the International League. Rickey promptly promoted him to the Dodgers in 1947.

"It won't be easy, Jack," Rickey said to his new star.

"There are fans and players who don't want to see black and white players on the same team. You will be taunted and insulted. I wouldn't be surprised if a couple of pitchers throw the ball at your head. And there is nothing you can do about it, Jack. You can't talk back and you can't fight back. You'll just have to take it."

"I'll do my best," Robinson replied quietly.

Jackie was really a second baseman, but the Dodgers had scrappy little Eddie Stanky in that position, so Robinson was switched to first base. Throughout the season, he had to grit his teeth and pretend he didn't hear the racial slurs coming from the dugouts and the stands. No matter what dirty name he was called, Robbie did not reply. Some opposing players threatened to go on strike if Robinson stepped onto their home field, but National League president Ford Frick put a stop to that. He promised to suspend every player who walked out, even if it meant wrecking the entire league. Baseball was the great *American* pastime, Frick said, and the game belonged to black and white players alike.

Robinson lived up to all expectations. He batted .296 and was voted Rookie of the Year. Now, in 1949, he would lead the National League in batting.

The fans, crowding into Ebbets Field, were buzzing about another human interest story: the great comeback of Joe DiMaggio. DiMaggio, who broke in with the Yankees in 1936, was nearing the end of his career by 1949. He had been bothered by a painful heel injury, and his heel was so sore he could not put his full weight on it. For the first half of the season, he sat on the bench, unable to play at all.

The Yankees were leading the league when they came to Boston on June 29th. But the Red Sox were hot. They

Philadelphia Phils' Andy Seminick, catching for the National League, lets American Leaguers' George Tebbett's high foul-pop get away from him for an error in the third inning of the 1949 all-star game.

had won four in a row, and if they could sweep the series, the Yanks would be in serious trouble. The day before the Red Sox series, DiMag had played in an exhibition game and found that his foot was well again. He told manager Casey Stengel he was ready to play.

In the first game, DiMaggio had a single and a homer. The Yanks won, 5–4. In the second game, DiMaggio hit two home runs and the Yanks came from behind to win again. In the third game, he hit another home run and the Yankees took that one, too. In that three-game series, DiMaggio hit four home runs and a single, driving in nine runs! Joe hadn't expected to play in the all-star game, but how could American League manager Lou Boudreau leave him out of the lineup? Big Joe was in the outfield that day.

On the mound for the National League was the Boston Braves' great left-hander, Warren Spahn. Together with right-hander Johnny Sain, he had pitched his team into the pennant. Boston fans had devised a little couplet in honor of their two pitchers:

> *Spahn and Sain*
> *Then two days of rain*

Spahn showed his stuff right away by striking out Dom DiMaggio. Then George Kell, the Detroit third baseman, banged a hopper to third. Eddie Kazak's throw was low and into the dirt, but a better fielding first baseman than Johnny Mize would have dug it out. The error was charged to Kazak.

When Spahn fanned the mighty Ted Williams, Kell stole second. Spahn should have been out of the inning with no runs. Instead, he had to face Joe DiMaggio. Joe lined out a base hit to score Kell. A walk to the next batter put runners on first and second. Then Eddie Robinson cracked one to the right side. Again, a good fielder might have come up with the ball, but Mize was just too slow. Another grounder was messed up by shortstop Peewee Reese. Catcher "Birdie" Tebbetts got a hit. Spahn struck out the next batter and walked dejectedly back to the dugout. The American League had scored four runs, none of them earned.

But the National League began pecking away at the enemy pitching. They got two runs in the first on Jackie

Robinson's double and Stan Musial's home run. They got another in the second on a walk, a single, a hit batter, and Don Newcombe's long fly which was caught near the wall. In the third, Robinson walked, took third on Musial's single, and scored, while Ralph Kiner was rapping into a double play. A hit by Mize and Eddie Kazak's single gave the Nationals a 5–4 lead.

As a defensive move, Gil Hodges replaced Mize at first when the fourth inning got under way. Hodges originally came to the Dodgers as a catcher, but Roy Campanella was just too good. Hodges was switched to first base, and became one of the finest fielders ever to play that position.

The St. Louis Cardinals' Stan Musial left, National League outfielder, is out at second base in the eighth inning of the 1949 all-star game.

BOX SCORES

AMERICAN	ab	r	h	rbi
D. DiMaggio, Bost. cf-rf	5	2	2	1
Raschi, NY p	1	0	0	0
Kell, Det. 3b	3	2	2	0
Dillinger, St. L. 3b	1	2	1	1
Williams, Bost. lf	2	1	0	0
Mitchell, Cleve. lf	1	0	1	0
J. DiMaggio, NY cf	4	1	2	3
Doby, Cleve. rf-cf	1	0	0	0
Joost, Phila. ss	2	1	1	2
Stephens, Bost. ss	2	0	0	0
E. Robinson, Wash. 1b	5	1	1	1
Goodman, Bost. 1b	0	0	0	0
Michaels, Chi. 2b	2	0	0	0
J. Gordon, Cleve. 2b	2	1	1	1
Tebbetts, Bost. c	2	0	2	1
Berra, NY c	3	0	0	0
Parnell, Bost. p	1	0	0	0
Trucks, Det. p	1	0	0	0
Brissie, Phila. p	1	0	0	0
Wertz, Det. rf	2	0	0	0
	41	11	13	10

NATIONAL	ab	r	h	rbi
Reese, B'klyn. ss	5	0	0	0
J. Robinson, B'klyn. 2b	4	3	1	0
Musial, St. L. cf-rf	4	1	3	2
Kiner, Pitt. lf	5	1	1	2
Mize, NY 1b	2	0	1	0
Hodges, B'klyn. 1b	3	1	1	0
Marshall, NY rf	1	1	0	0
Bickford, Bost. p	0	0	0	0
Thomson, NY	1	0	0	0
Pollet, St. L.	0	0	0	0
Blackwell, Cin. p	0	0	0	0
Slaughter, St. L. rf	1	0	0	0
Roe, B'klyn. p	0	0	0	0
Kazak, St. L. 3b	2	0	2	1
S. Gordon, NY 3b	2	0	1	0
Seminick, Phila. c	1	0	0	0
Campanella, B'klyn. c	2	0	0	0
Spahn, Bost. p	0	0	0	0
Newcombe, B'klyn. p	1	0	0	1
Schoendienst, St. L.	1	0	1	0
Munger, St. L. p	0	0	0	0
Pafko, Chi. cf	2	0	1	0
	37	7	12	6

LINE SCORE

					R	H	E
American	400	202	300	=	11	13	1
National	212	002	000	=	7	12	5

Errors: Mitchell, Reese, Marshall, Kazak, Seminick, Campanella. Two-base hits: J. Robinson, Tebbetts, S. Gordon, D. DiMaggio, J. DiMaggio, J. Gordon, Mitchell. Home runs: Musial, Kiner. Stolen base: Kell. Double plays (3). Left on base: American 8, National 12. Bases on balls: off Spahn 2; off Parnell 1; off Newcombe 1; off Trucks 2; off Munger 1; off Bickford 1; off Brissie 2; off Raschi 3. Struck out: by Spahn 3; by Parnell 1; by Brissie 1; by Blackwell 2; by Raschi 1. Hits: off Spahn 4 in 1 1/3; off Parnell 3 in 1; off Newcombe 3 in 2 2/3; off Trucks 3 in 2; off Munger 0 in 1; off Bickford 2 in 1; off Brissie 5 in 3; off Pollet 4 in 1; off Blackwell 0 in 1; off Roe 0 in 1; off Raschi 1 in 3. Hit by pitcher: by Parnell 1. Winning pitcher—Trucks. Losing pitcher—Newcombe. Umpires: Barlick, Hubbard, Gore, Summers, Ballanfant, Frieve.

There were two runners on base and two out when Eddie Joost, the Philadelphia shortstop, came to bat. Pitcher Don Newcombe broke off a curve that fooled Joost. He swung at it, and nicked the ball with the very edge of his bat. The ball went slithering and veering at a crazy angle between first and seond. Hodges went for it, trying to make a bare-handed stab. The ball kept spinning and slicing, hitting Hodges on the fingers and going into right field. Both runners scored on the freak hit. The score was 6–5, in favor of the American League.

In the sixth, the Americans increased their lead to 8–5 when Dom DiMaggio doubled, Kell walked, and big Joe DiMaggio chased them both home with a double to left-center. Once again, the Nationals struck back as Kiner hit one into the seats with Robinson on base. That made the score 8–7.

Then the American League put the game out of reach against Howie Pollet of the St. Louis Cardinals. They sandwiched two doubles around two singles for three more runs. The final score was 11–7.

It had been one of the sloppiest games ever played by an all-star team. The National League committed five errors and messed up a few plays that didn't show in the box score. The damage might have been worse, but Andy Pafko of the Cubs made a spectacular sliding catch on a sinking line drive off the bat of Vic Wertz to stop further scoring. It was one of the few good fielding plays of the game. Another fine catch was made by Ted Williams on Newcombe's long fly in the second inning.

But, sloppy game or not, 1949's contest proved that black players were worthy of being called all-stars. They were in major league baseball to stay.

July 11, 1950—
Comiskey Park,
Chicago

There were still only sixteen major-league teams in 1950. Each home park had already been the site of one all-star game. So, the seventeenth game returned to Chicago's Comiskey Park—the site of the first all-star game. The 46, 127 fans who paid to see the game were glad to welcome the all-star back.

Burt Shotton, who managed the Brooklyn Dodgers when they won a pennant in 1949, told sportswriters he wasn't too happy with the outfielders the fans had selected for him. Although they were outstanding sluggers—Hank Sauer of the Cubs, Enos Slaughter of the Cardinals, and Ralph Kiner of Pittsburgh—none of them was a center fielder. Why, Shotton asked sportswriters, didn't they give him his own Duke Snider, who patrolled center for the Dodgers? The graceful Snider could cover ground and had a strong arm. Slaughter could run fairly well, but Kiner and Sauer were slow. However, Slaughter was a right fielder. He had played a few games in center, but that was a long time ago. Still, there was no one else Shotton could use, at least for the first three innings. That was one of the all-star game rules. Every starter, except the pitcher, had to play at least three innings unless he was injured.

Casey Stengel, managing an all-star team for the first time, told everybody how happy he was. "I never thought I'd have so many good players on my team," he said in his froggy voice. "I'm not sure I know how to manage 'em."

Shotten chose rookie right-hander Robin Roberts, of the Philadelphia Phillies, to start the game. Roberts had a blazing fast ball—he would win twenty games in 1950 and help the Phils to win the National League pennant. But at first, he had difficulties. Roberts would start to tire in the late innings. Although he was a strong young man, his fast ball would lose its zing. However, it wasn't hard to find out what was wrong with Roberts. He was working too fast. Immediately after a pitch, he wanted the catcher to return the ball to him. Then he would get the sign and deliver the next pitch right away. He wasn't pacing himself right.

The Philadelphia coaches devised a way for Roberts to take a little rest between pitches. When the catcher returned the ball to him, he would walk behind the mound. Then he would adjust his pants legs, smooth down his shirt, take off his cap, brush back his hair, hitch up his pants again, and take a deep breath. That little twenty- or thirty-second breather seemed to work wonders. The players and fans kidded him good-naturedly, asking why he didn't finish dressing in the locker room. But Roberts took the ribbing and kept on winning.

Roberts got through the first two innings without being scored on, but it took a nice catch by Enos Slaughter to keep the American League at bay. In the second inning, Walt Dropo, the huge Red Sox first baseman, banged a

Victorious National Leaguers congratulate Ewell Blackwell, Cincinnati pitcher, in the 1950 all-star game that lasted for fourteen innings before the American Leaguers bowed, 4–3.

415-foot shot to deepest center. "Country" Slaughter ran back about a hundred feet and flagged it down.

Vic Raschi, the "Springfield Rifle," who pitched for the Yankees, got by the first inning, but he, too, needed a super catch. Ralph Kiner smashed one out to deep left center. Ted Williams raced back to the barrier and made a one-handed catch. He crashed into the fence on his left elbow and grimaced with pain. But after rubbing his elbow for a minute or two, he waved for the game to go on.

Raschi wasn't quite as lucky in the second inning. Jackie Robinson helped himself to a base hit, and "Country" Slaughter bashed a fast ball to left center for a triple, scoring Robinson. A long fly by Sauer fetched Slaughter home.

Again, in the third inning, Williams took a sure base hit away from Kiner. This time he galloped in and made a shoestring catch on a sinking line drive.

The American League was trailing by 2–0 when they took their licks in the bottom of the third. Cass Michaels, the Washington second baseman, pinch hit for Raschi and came up with a ground-rule double. Little Phil "Scooter" Rizzuto, one of baseball's greatest bunters, dropped a beauty along the inside of the third-base path. There was nothing "Puddin'head" Jones could do but let it roll and hope it went foul. But the ball stayed fair. Michaels reached third, and Rizzuto had himself a bunt single. Michaels scored on George Kell's long sacrifice fly to center. The outfielders on both teams were getting a good workout in the early innings.

With a little bit of luck, the Americans took the lead in the bottom of the fifth. Bob Lemon opened with a walk, then Larry Doby sent a high bouncer over the mound. It wasn't a hard-hit ball, but nobody could get to it. Jackie Robinson reached out and got his glove on the ball momentarily, but it got away and trickled slowly into the outfield. Lemon reached third, and Doby hustled the "seeing-eye grounder" into a double. Once more, George Kell drove in a run with a long fly to center. Ted Williams got Doby across with a base hit.

The teams played scoreless ball through the sixth, seventh, and eighth innings. Ted Gray, a Detroit pitcher, was on the hill in the top of the ninth. Ralph Kiner came to bat and hit one out of the park, where an outfielder couldn't rob him. That tied the score. Larry Jansen, of the

New York Giants, was pitching strongly, and the American League batters couldn't dent the plate. For the first time, an all-star game went into extra innings.

The tenth inning was scoreless. So were the eleventh, twelfth, and thirteenth. Jansen gave way to Ewell "The Whip" Blackwell in the twelfth after five innings of one-hit pitching. Blackwell had a dazzling fast ball, which he threw side-arm. To a right-handed batter, the ball seemed to be coming from third base. When Blackwell had good control—which was very often—the ball hit the inside corner of the plate to left-handed hitters. They usually hit the ball off the handle of the bat. The American Leaguers couldn't do much with Blackwell, either.

Red Schoendienst, right, after his home run that won the fourteenth inning in the 1950 all-star game.

BOX SCORES

AMERICAN

	ab	r	h	rbi
Rizzuto, NY ss	6	0	2	0
Doby, Cleve. cf	6	1	2	0
Kell, Det. 3b	6	0	0	2
Williams, Bost. lf	4	0	1	1
D. DiMaggio, Bost. lf	2	0	0	0
Dropo, Bost. 1b	3	0	1	0
Fain, Phila. 1b	3	0	1	0
Evers, Det. rf	2	0	0	0
J. DiMaggio, NY rf	3	0	0	0
Berra, NY c	2	0	0	0
Hegan, Cleve. c	3	0	0	0
Doerr, Bost. 2b	3	0	0	0
Coleman, NY 2b	2	0	0	0
Raschi, NY p	0	0	0	0
Michaels, Wash.	1	1	1	0
Lemon, Cleve. p	0	1	0	0
Houtteman, Det. p	1	0	0	0
Reynolds, NY p	1	0	0	0
Henrich, NY	1	0	0	0
Gray, Det. p	0	0	0	0
Feller, Cleve. p	0	0	0	0
	49	3	8	3

NATIONAL

	ab	r	h	rbi
Jones, Phila. 3b	7	0	1	0
Kiner, Pitts. lf	6	1	2	1
Musial, St. L. 1b	5	0	0	0
Robinson, B'klyn. 2b	4	1	1	0
Wyrostek, Cin. rf	2	0	0	0
Slaughter, St. L. cf-rf	4	1	2	1
Schoendienst, St. L. 2b	1	1	1	1
Sauer, Chi. rf	2	0	0	1
Pafko, Chi. rf	4	0	2	0
Campanella, B'klyn. c	6	0	0	0
Marion, St. L. ss	2	0	0	0
Konstanty, Phila. p	0	0	0	0
Jansen, NY p	2	0	0	0
Snider, B'klyn.	1	0	0	0
Blackwell, Cin. p	1	0	0	0
Roberts, Phila. p	1	0	0	0
Newcombe, B'klyn. p	0	0	0	0
Sisler, Phila.	1	0	1	0
Reese, B'klyn. ss	3	0	0	0
	52	4	10	4

LINE SCORE

								R	H	E
National	020	000	001	000	01	=		4	10	0
American	001	020	000	000	00	=		3	8	1

Error: Coleman. Two-base hits: Michaels, Doby, Kiner. Three-base hits: Slaughter, Dropo. Home runs: Kiner, Schoendienst. Left on base: National 9; American 8. Double plays (2). Hits: off Raschi 2 in 3 innings; off Roberts 3 in 3; off Newcombe 0 in 1; off Lemon 1 in 3; off Konstanty 0 in 1; off Houtteman 3 in 3; off Jansen 1 in 5; off Reynolds 1 in 3; off Blackwell 1 in 3; off Gray 3 in 1 1/3; off Feller 0 in 2/3. Bases on balls: off Roberts 1; off Newcombe 1; off Houtteman 1; off Reynolds 1; off Feller 1. Struck out: by Raschi 1; by Roberts 1; by Lemon 2; by Newcombe 1; by Konstanty 2; by Jansen 6; by Reynolds 2; by Blackwell 2; by Gray 1; by Feller 1. Wild pitch: Roberts. Passed ball: Hegan. Winning pitcher—Blackwell. Losing pitcher—Gray. Umpires: McGowan, Pinelli, Rommel, Conlan, Stevens, Robb.

Art Houtteman of Detroit was pitching when Red Schoendienst, the switch-hitting second baseman, stepped in. Schoendienst wasn't known as a home-run hitter, especially batting lefty. But Houtteman made one pitch too good, and the redhead lost it in the stands. Blackwell held the Americans in check in the bottom of the fourteenth. It was all over. The National League had won, 4–3.

There had been two home runs hit in the 1950 all-star game. Ironically, both had come off Detroit pitching. It proved to be a costly game for Ted Williams and the Boston Red Sox. When Williams came out of the game, he went to the dressing room. His elbow had begun to swell up. The trainer massaged it for a while, but the pain did not go away. Williams caught an early plane for home and consulted a doctor. X-rays showed bone damage. An operation was performed immediately, and the surgeon removed seven bone chips from Williams's elbow. Williams was out of action for most of the remainder of the season. He played a total of eighty-seven games and his average slumped to .317.

Also slightly injured in the game was Joe DiMaggio. He had been bothered by leg injuries and was playing only because Casey Stengel wanted to show him off to the fans. It would have been wiser to have left Joe on the bench. He hit into a double play, but always hustling, he tried to beat the throw to first. The speed just wasn't there any longer. He strained a muscle in his groin and had to rest for a few days.

All-star games could be exciting. They could also be disasters for managers who lost their best players as a result of the 1950 game.

July 13, 1954—
Municipal Stadium,
Cleveland

In 1949, Casey Stengel's Yankees won the American League pennant and the World Series as well. Therefore, Casey managed the all-star team in 1950. The American League lost, 4–3. The same thing happened during the 1950 season. Stengel's Yanks won everything in sight, but in 1951, the American League all-stars lost again, 8–3. History repeated itself in the 1951, 1952, and 1953 seasons. Casey Stengel's teams were always world champions, but "The Ol' Perfessor" couldn't break the jinx. He had won five World Series, but lost four all-star games.

"Maybe this is the year," he told sportswriters in Cleveland. "I can't keep losin' 'em forever."

"Why not?" one writer joked. "You keep winning the World Series every year."

"Then how come I manage so good in the regular season and I'm so bad in the all-star games?" Casey asked, a twinkle in his eyes.

The real answer was that anything could happen in a single game. Over a season, the Yankees could hit a losing streak, then start winning again. But an all-star contest was like a one-game series. The loser had no opportunity to get even until the next year.

Both Casey and his rival, Walter Alston, had a few problem players. Al Rosen, the Cleveland slugger who played first or third base, had a bad finger. Yogi Berra's left wrist was sore as a result of having been hit by a pitch. And, while shagging outfield flies, pitcher Bob Turley ran into a wire fence and ended up with a scrape over his right eye.

Among Alston's charges, Duke Snider was bothered by twinges in his elbow, Jackie Robinson had a bad heel and ankle, and Roy Campanella's left hand was tender and sore. Still, everybody except Turley was more or less able-bodied and wanted to play.

For the fourth time in five years, Robin Roberts started for the National League. But it was soon apparent that the ace right-hander didn't have his stuff. The American League didn't score in the first inning, although Roberts yielded a single and a walk. Nor did they get a run in the second when they got another base hit. Roberts seemed to lead a charmed life.

His luck ran out in the third. Minnie Minoso and Bobby Avila got on base, but Mantle and Berra were retired. Al Rosen came to bat. Roberts had already struck him out once, but he wouldn't do it this time. Rosen smashed one deep over the left center wall. A moment later, Ray Boone, the Detroit third baseman, hit one that landed only a foot to the side of Rosen's blast. Two fat pitches—bang—bang!—and the American League had a 4–0 lead.

Sandy Consuegra of the White Sox was pitching for

National League shortstop Alvin Dark lunges in vain for Nelson Fox's blooper single past second in the eighth inning of the 1954 all-star game.

Red Schoendienst, left, National League infielder, rolls in the dust after being tagged out on an attempted steal of home in the eighth inning of the 1954 all-star game. Yogi Berra, American League catcher, is also floored after taking pitcher Dean Stone's peg and making the tag on Schoendienst.

Stengel's forces at the start of the fourth. He got one batter out. By the time the dust had settled, Consuegra was out of the game. Snider, Musial, Ted Kluszewski, and Ray Jablonski, the St. Louis third baseman, hit successive singles. Jackie Robinson's double and Don Mueller's pinch two-bagger made it 5–4 in favor of the Nationals.

When the American League tied the score at 5–all, the fans knew it was going to be raining base hits that afternoon. They were right. Duke Snider got another hit. Then Ted Kluszewski, whose arms looked like tree trunks, powered the ball over the right field fence to make it 7–5. This was answered by Yogi Berra's hit and Al Rosen's second home run of the day—not bad hitting for a player whose finger was hurt.

The American League inched ahead on a walk to Ted Williams and hits by Minoso and Bobby Avila. But the Nationals were also playing long-ball. Mays singled, and Gus Bell hit the ball out to give the Nationals the lead in the eighth inning. It looked like a big rally was in the works when Red Schoendienst got on via an error and was pushed around to third base. Dean Stone, a young hurler, was brought in to pitch to Snider, who already had a couple of hits in the game. Red Schoendienst watched Stone take his warm-up pitches and decided he could steal home on the kid. As Stone began to pitch, Schoendienst broke for the plate. Stone recovered and threw hurriedly to Berra, who put the tag on Red.

Immediately, coaches Leo Durocher and Charlie Grimm came tearing over to plate umpire Bill Stewart to protest. They claimed that Stone had balked. "Leo the Lip" put on his usual show, kicking the dirt and waving his arms, but no player ever wins an argument with an umpire.

Leo Durocher, left, speaks his mind, as Charlie Grimm, center, protests plate umpire Bill Stewart's decision during the 1954 all-star game.

Schoendienst was out, the side was retired, the Nationals led, 9–8, and it was "Play ball!"

When Larry Doby pinch hit for Stone and hit a home run, it marked the sixth time a player had given the bleacher fans a souvenir. Four of the homers had come off American League bats.

The rally continued, as Berra and Mantle got hits and Rosen walked to load the bases. Little Nellie Fox, who played second base for the White Sox, stepped to the plate. He was almost fooled by a curve, but managed to get a piece of the pitch. The ball looped lazily over the infield while the shortstop, the second baseman, and the center fielder tried desperately to reach it. Then it just plopped on the grass as two runs scored to put the Americans in the lead, 11–9. That was the final score.

39

In a way, it was a strange ball game. Two-base hits and home runs had been flying through the air regularly, but it was a dinky little nubber that won the game. Another oddity was the fact that Dean Stone was the winning pitcher. He was on the hill when Schoendienst tried to steal and failed. Snider, whom he was facing, didn't have his full turn at bat. Therefore, Dean Stone won a ball game without retiring a single batter!

As for Stengel, at long last he had an all-star victory. But, as he later learned to his regret, there is always a fly in the ointment somewhere. For, in 1954, the Cleveland Indians won the American League pennant and the World Series, too.

"Well," Casey shrugged after the season was over, "I guess you can't have everything."

The crucial play in the eighth inning of the 1954 all-star game.

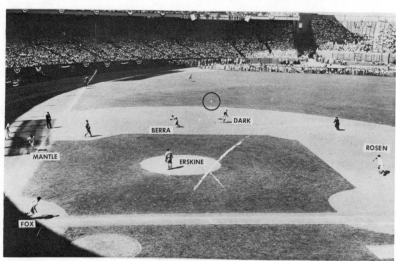

BOX SCORES

AMERICAN

	ab	r	h	rbi
Minoso, Chi. lf-rf	4	1	2	0
Piersall, Bost. rf	0	0	0	0
Avila, Cleve. 2b	3	1	3	2
Keegan, Chi. p	0	0	0	0
Stone, Wash. p	0	0	0	0
Doby, Cleve. cf	1	1	1	1
Trucks, Chi. p	0	0	0	0
Mantle, NY cf	5	1	2	0
Berra, NY c	4	2	2	0
Rosen, Cleve. 1b-3b	4	2	3	5
Boone, Cleve. 3b	4	1	1	1
Vernon, Wash. 1b	1	0	0	0
Bauer, NY rf	2	0	1	0
Porterfield, Wash. p	1	0	0	0
Fox, Chi. 2b	2	0	1	2
Carrasquel, Chi. ss	5	1	1	0
Ford, NY p	1	0	0	0
Conseguera, Chi. p	0	0	0	0
Lemon, Cleve. p	0	0	0	0
Williams, Bost. lf	2	1	0	0
Noren, NY lf	0	0	0	0
	39	11	17	11

NATIONAL

	ab	r	h	rbi
Hamner, Phil. 2b	3	0	0	0
Schoendienst, St. L. 2b	2	0	0	0
Dark, NY ss	5	0	1	0
Snider, B'klyn. cf-rf	4	2	3	0
Musial, St. L. rf-lf	5	1	2	0
Kluszewski, Cin. 1b	4	2	2	3
Hodges, B'klyn. 1b	1	0	0	0
Jablonski, St. L. 3b	3	1	1	1
Jackson, Chi. 3b	2	0	0	0
Robinson, B'klyn. lf	2	1	1	2
Mays, NY cf	2	1	1	0
Campanella, B'klyn. c	3	0	1	0
Burgess, Phila. c	0	0	0	0
Roberts, Phila. p	1	0	0	0
Mueller, NY	1	0	1	1
Antonelli, NY p	0	0	0	0
Thomas, Pitt.	1	0	0	0
Spahn, Mil. p	0	0	0	0
Grissom, NY p	0	0	0	0
Bell, Cin.	1	1	1	2
Conley, Mil. p	0	0	0	0
Erskine, B'klyn. p	0	0	0	0
	40	9	14	9

LINE SCORE

				R	H	E
National	000	520	020 =	9	14	0
American	004	121	03x =	11	17	1

Error: Minoso. Two-base hits: Robinson, Mueller, Snider. Home runs: Rosen (2), Boone, Kluszewski, Bell, Doby. Double play (1). Left on base: National 6, American 9. Bases on balls: off Roberts 2, off Spahn 1, off Conley 1, off Ford 1, off Trucks 1. Struck out: by Roberts 5, by Antonelli 2, by Grissom 2, by Erskine 1, by Porterfield 1. Hits: off Ford 1 in 3 innings; off Conseguera 5 in 1/3; off Lemon 2 in 2 1/3; off Porterfield 4 in 2; off Keegan 3 in 2/3; off Stone 0 in 1/3; off Trucks 0 in 1; off Roberts 5 in 3, off Antonelli 4 in 2; off Spahn 4 in 2/3; off Grissom 0 in 1 1/3; off Conley 3 in 1/3. Winning pitcher—Stone. Losing pitcher—Conley. Umpires: Rommel, Ballanfant, Honochick, Stewart, Gorman, Paparella.

July 9, 1957—
Busch Stadium,
St. Louis

For the seventh time in eight years, Casey Stengel was at the helm when the American League team took the field. And, as was so often the case, his rival was Walter Alston of the Dodgers. But that was the last year for the team in Brooklyn. After the season was over, the team would shift to Los Angeles.

To the press and the public, Casey Stengel was a combination of clown and genius. Sportswriters never tired of interviewing him. He was funny without trying to be, and he talked in circles so that few really understood what he was saying. After a while, the reporters said that Casey was talking "Stengelese," which was almost a language of its own.

One of the best stories about Casey concerned an incident that took place when he was playing for the Pittsburgh Pirates in 1918. The previous year, Casey had played for the Dodgers, but he got into a salary dispute with the management and was traded. One day, when the Pirates were playing in Brooklyn, a Pittsburgh pitcher managed to capture a sparrow. Stengel saw it happen, and asked the pitcher for the bird. He placed it carefully under his cap. When Casey came to bat, the Brooklyn fans, who had always liked him, began to cheer. Casey acknowledged the greeting by bowing and tipping his cap, whereupon the bird flew off the top of his head to freedom.

Wilbert Robinson, the manager of the Dodgers, remarked at the time, "I always knew Stengel had birds in his top story."

Gus Bell of the Cincinnati Reds slices a foul in the ninth inning of the 1957 all-star game. He later drew a base on balls.

Yet Stengel was a keen judge of baseball players. Few others knew managing strategy as he did. It was Casey who brought the system of platooning players to a high art. Unfortunately, during the early years of his managing career, he was stuck with terrible teams. He managed the Brooklyn Dodgers for a while, but they usually finished in sixth place. He also managed the Boston Braves with no better luck.

"There are two types of ball players," Stengel told reporters. "One type is the professionals. They can execute the plays. The other type is the ribbon clerks. They should look for another line of work."

Almost everyone was surprised when Stengel was named to manage the Yankees in 1949. He had never proved himself a winning major league manager. However, Casey never had as many fine players as the Yankees provided for him. As the years passed, he found himself piloting such magnificent stars as Joe DiMaggio, Tommy Henrich, Mickey Mantle, Yogi Berra, Tony Kubek, Bill Skowron, Gil McDougald, Vic Raschi, Allie Reynolds and many, many more.

There were only two things Casey was unhappy about when the 1957 game got under way. First, out of six attempts, he had managed to win only one all-star game, in 1954. Secondly, he did not approve of some of the players the fans had chosen for him.

The fans had voted Vic Wertz to play first base. Wertz was slumping badly at the plate, and had tailed off to a .295 average. A far better choice would have been Stengel's Bill Skowron, who was slugging away at .332. Nor did Casey want Harvey Kuenn to play short. In fact, Kuenn was no longer a shortstop. He was now playing third base.

Vic Wertz hits a single in the second inning of the 1957 all-star game.

Why did the fans switch him back to a position his own
team felt he could no longer play? The shortstop should
have been Gil McDougald, who was covering the position
well and batting .312. Also, why was George Kell at third?
He was batting only .281. Didn't the fans know that Frank
Malzone of the Red Sox was wielding a hot bat, with a .327
average? But there was nothing Casey could do, at least for
the first three innings.

Walter Alston was not exactly cheering for his National League team, either. The fault lay with the Cincinnati fans. They had really stuffed the ballot boxes. Almost
the entire Reds team had been selected. Then Commis-

sioner Ford Frick stepped in. He said it would be all right to start five Cincinnati players: Johnny Temple at second; Roy McMillan at short; Don Hoak at third; Frank Robinson in left field; and Ed Bailey behind the plate. But he ordered Stan Musial (hitting .341) to play first base, Willie Mays (.308) to play center, and Hank Aaron (.347) to play right field.

The American League broke out on top in the second inning. With lefty Curt Simmons on the mound, the switch-hitting Mickey Mantle came to the plate and batted right-handed. The left side of the infield played deep. Mantle topped a sinker and dribbled it along the third base line. It went for an infield hit. Ted Williams walked. Vic Wertz snapped out of his slump with a sliced single, scoring Mantle. Berra walked. Out came Simmons and in went Lew Burdette of the Milwaukee Braves. Burdette retired two batters, but Kuenn walked for the second run. Thus, the two batters Stengel did not want in the lineup each batted in a run.

But that did not deter Casey. After the first three innings were over, he yanked Wertz, Kuenn, and Kell, and substituted Skowron, McDougald, and Malzone. Skowron made the move look good in the sixth inning, when he banged a double and scored on teammate Yogi Berra's single. Oddly, it was the first run batted in for Berra in nine all-star games. He had been to bat twenty-eight times during that time.

In the seventh inning, the selections of both Commissioner Frick and the Cincinnati fans looked very good. Frick's sub, Willie Mays, rapped out a single. So did Redleg Ed Bailey, the fans' choice. Cincinnati outfielder Gus Bell batted for teammate Frank Robinson and hit a two-bagger, scoring both runners. The American League's lead was cut to 3–2.

In the ninth, it appeared that the American League had iced the game. The surge began with a hit and an error by Red Schoendienst, who had replaced Johnny Temple at second. Nellie Fox moved up both runners with a neat bunt. Al Kaline singled home both runners. A moment later, Kaline was plated by Minnie Minoso's double. With the score 6–2, some of the fans headed for the exits to beat the traffic rush. They made a big mistake.

Stan "The Man" Musial opened the bottom of the

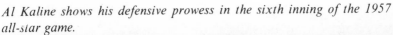

Al Kaline shows his defensive prowess in the sixth inning of the 1957 all-star game.

ninth with a walk off left-hander Billy Pierce. Willie Mays, playing with a bruised instep, sliced a wrong-way triple down the right field line to score Musial. Then Mays came in on a wild pitch. Pinch hitter Hank Foiles, the Pittsburgh catcher, renewed the attack with a single, and Gus Bell drew a pass. Stengel took out Pierce in favor of Don Mossi, a relief specialist. This strategy paid off when Eddie Mathews was struck out. But Ernie Banks singled past third, scoring Foiles. However, Bell rounded second and dashed for third. Then came the key play.

Out in left field, the ball was picked up by Minnie Minoso (his full name was actually Saturnino Orestes Arrieta Armas Minoso), who fired the ball to Malzone. Bell was out by an eyelash.

Casey yanked Mossi in favor of Yankee pitcher Bob Grim. Alston countered with Gil Hodges. Hodges cracked a vicious hooking line drive toward the left field corner. Minoso came up with his second sparkling play in succession. Sprinting at top speed, Minoso reached out to make a gloved-hand catch just as the ball was about to go by. That was the final out of the game. The American League won, 6–5, and Casey Stengel had his second all-star victory.

Sportswriters agreed that it had been a well-played game and that the finish was exciting. But they also noted that Cincinnati fans had overlooked the basic reason for the game: to field two teams composed of the best players from each league. Something would have to be done to prevent that from happening in the future.

BOX SCORES

AMERICAN

	ab	r	h	rbi
Kuenn, Det. ss	2	0	0	1
McDougald, NY ss	2	1	0	0
Fox, Chi. 2b	4	0	0	0
Kaline, Det. rf	5	1	2	2
Mantle, NY cf	4	1	1	0
Williams, Bost. lf	3	1	0	0
Minoso, Chi. lf	1	0	1	1
Wertz, Cleve. 1b	2	0	1	1
Skowron, NY 1b	3	1	2	0
Berra, NY c	3	0	1	1
Kell, Balt. 3b	2	0	0	0
Malzone, Bost. 3b	2	0	0	0
Bunning, Det. p	1	0	0	0
Maxwell, Det.	1	0	1	0
Loes, Balt. p	1	0	0	0
Wynn, Cleve. p	0	0	0	0
Pierce, Chi. p	1	1	1	0
Mossi, Cleve. p	0	0	0	0
Grim, NY p	0	0	0	0
	37	6	10	6

NATIONAL

	ab	r	h	rbi
Temple, Cin. 2b	2	0	0	0
Schoendienst, Mil. 2b	2	0	0	0
Aaron, Mil. rf	4	0	1	0
Musial, St. L. 1b	3	1	1	0
Mays, NY cf	4	2	2	1
Bailey, Cin. c	3	1	1	0
Foiles, Pitt.	1	1	1	0
Robinson, Cin. lf	2	0	1	0
Bell, Cin. lf	1	0	1	2
Hoak, Cin. 3b	1	0	0	0
Mathews, Mil. 3b	3	0	0	0
McMillan, Cin. ss	1	0	0	0
Banks, Chi. ss	3	0	1	1
Simmons, Phil. p	0	0	0	0
Burdette, Mil. p	1	0	0	0
Sanford, Phil. p	0	0	0	0
Moon, St. L.	1	0	0	0
Jackson, St. L. p	0	0	0	0
Cimoli, B'klyn.	1	0	0	0
Labine, B'klyn. p	0	0	0	0
Hodges, B'klyn.	1	0	0	0
	34	5	9	4

LINE SCORE

				R	H	E
American	020	001	003 =	6	10	0
National	000	000	203 =	5	9	1

Error: Schoendienst. Two-base hits: Musial, Skowron, Bell, Minoso. Three-base hits: Mays. Sacrifice: Fox. Double plays (1). Left on base: American 9, National 4. Bases on balls: off Simmons 2, off Burdette 1, off Jackson 1, off Loes 1, off Pierce 2. Struck out: by Bunning 1, by Loes 1, by Pierce 3, by Labine 1, by Mossi 1. Hits: off Simmons 2 in 1 inning; off Bunning 0 in 3; off Burdette 2 in 4; off Sanford 2 in 1; off Loes 3 in 3; off Wynn 3 in 1/3; off Jackson 1 in 2; off Labine 3 in 1; off Pierce 3 in 1 2/3; off Mossi 1 in 2/3; off Grim 0 in 1/3. Wild pitch: Sanford, Pierce. Winning pitcher—Bunning. Losing pitcher—Simmons. Umpires. Dascoli, Napp, Dixon, Stevens, Landes, Chylak.

July 8, 1958—
Memorial Stadium,
Baltimore

The attempt by Cincinnati fans to stuff the ballot boxes backfired against all fans. The rules for selecting players for the 1958 all-star game were changed, so that the fans had no voice at all.

Now the players in each league chose the team to represent them. However, they were not permitted to vote for anyone from their own team. For instance, no one on the Yankees could vote for Mickey Mantle, because he, too, was a Yankee. But it was generally agreed that players on other teams would surely vote for Mantle (they did), and, in case of a close vote, probably the runner-up would also make the team via the manager's choice.

One of the players selected was Stan Musial. It was his fifteenth all-star game. Even before 1958, Musial held several all-star records. He had the most hits, sixteen; the most home runs, five; the most total bases, thirty-three. Musial had been a left-handed pitcher at one time, but when he hurt his arm, he realized his pitching days were over. He switched over to the outfield, worked his way through the minors, and became one of baseball's Hall of Fame outfielders (he also played first base late in his career).

Musial batted with a closed stance, with his feet fairly close together. He had a slight crouch, and his chin almost rested on his right shoulder. "Stan looks like a man peering over his shoulder to see if the bus is coming," one sportswriter wrote. Musial described himself as "Just a li'l ol' singles hitter."

Regardless of his stance, Stan Musial was one of baseball's all-time great batters. He arrived in St. Louis at

Leftfielder Bob Cerv, of the American League, robs Dell Crandall and a fan of the ball as he crashes into the left field wall during the sixth inning of the all-star game.

the end of the 1941 season, and for years afterward, he was one of the mainstays of the Cardinals' batting order. If there was one batter that National League pitchers did *not* want to see in a clutch situation, it was Musial.

Another old-timer in the game was Boston's Ted Williams. Musial would have been the first to admit that perhaps some of his all-star records would have been surpassed by the Boston slugger. Unfortunately, two wars interfered. When the conflict broke out in Korea, Williams was called back to active duty. He flew thirty-nine combat missions in 1952. His plane was hit twice by enemy fire. Williams was awarded three Air Force medals for his service with the United States Marines. Counting World War II, he had spent five years in the service.

Surely he would have been voted to the all-star team, and he would have hit home runs, and had many total bases. Yet Williams never complained. In his prime, he had been the finest hitter in baseball. Everyone admitted it, even some of the Boston sportswriters who did not like him. When they asked him personal questions about his private life, Ted would tell them bluntly that what he did off the field was none of their business. The writers, accustomed to jokes and evasions in answer to such questions, described Williams as a "loner," and wrote that perhaps success was going to his head.

Probably the finest day of Ted Williams's career was the last day of the 1941 season. For most of the year, he had been batting just over .400. Fans were wondering if he could keep it up. Only seven major leaguers in history had done that—Ty Cobb, Rogers Hornsby, Napoleon Lajoie, Harry Heilmann, George Sisler, "Shoeless" Joe Jackson, and Bill Terry.

Luis Aparicio, of the American League, slides into home plate in the second inning of the 1958 all-star game.

In the final week, Williams dropped down to .399. But on the final day, the Red Sox played a doubleheader against the Philadelphia Athletics. In his first at bat, Ted cracked a single. His next time up, he hit a home run. Manager Joe Cronin suggested that he sit down, because he had his .400 average locked up.

"No," Ted said. "Either I can hit .400 for a whole season or I can't. I'm going to find out."

In his next two trips, he got two more hits. And he played in the second game as well, banging out two more base hits. He finished the season at .406. Yes, Ted Williams was always worthy of playing on an all-star team.

The 1958 all-star game was important because it was the silver anniversary of the series. Actually, the games had begun twenty-six years ago, but one game had not been played during World War II. Casey Stengel was back as the

American League manager. Fred Haney was managing the National League, after leading the Milwaukee Braves to the flag the previous year.

It was a surprise move to have a hitter like Willie Mays in the leadoff spot. Haney's explanation for that was simple. "Mays is a good man to start off an inning. Besides, I intend to pinch hit for the pitcher, and I'll be using a good batter. Maybe he'll get on. And Mays is just as good when he comes to bat with a man on base."

Mays proved Haney to be a genius right away. His bouncer toward third hit the bag and went for a single. One out later, Musial singled on a hit-and-run play, sending Mays to third. He scored on Hank Aaron's long fly to center.

At this point, Yankee starting pitcher Bob Turley suddenly lost his control. He hit Ernie Banks and walked Frank Thomas to load the bases. Then he let fly a wild pitch, and Musial scored. The Nationals led, 2–0, at the end of the first half-inning.

The Americans looked like they might score a few runs themselves on an error by Cub shortstop Ernie Banks and Mantle's long single. But Jackie Jensen bounced into a rally-killing 4–6–3 double play. A run scored, but that was all.

Turley's wildness continued in the second inning. He walked the opposing pitcher, but Willie Mays hit into a forceout. However, Mays promptly stole second, and continued on to third when catcher Gus Triandos's throw went into center field. He scored on Bob Skinner's single.

Once more, the American League got a run back; the scoring hit was a single by Nellie Fox. Fox seldom hit the long ball. Most of his safeties dropped just over the infield.

But, with men in scoring position, he was as dangerous as any slugger.

Pittsburgh's Bob Friend was on the mound in the fifth inning. Friend had a fine sinker, which he could use effectively with men on base. But he got into a jam instantly. Pinch hitter Mickey Vernon of Cleveland singled, Nellie Fox chipped in with his second hit, and Mantle walked to load the bases. With nobody out, Jackie Jensen stepped in. Jensen had already hit into one double play. His trouble was that he tried to pull every pitch to left field. He could not, or would not, hit the low outside pitch to right field. As a result, he often hit ground balls to the infield.

Friend threw his sinking, fast ball. Jensen sent a grounder up the middle. Friend lunged for the ball but just missed it. Second baseman Bill Mazeroski fielded the ball and threw Jensen out at first, but Vernon scored. Had Friend been able to come up with the ball, he could have easily started a pitcher-catcher-first double play. He failed to come up with the ball by a matter of an inch or two. But Friend still was in control of the situation. He walked Bob Cerv to load the bases, then induced Bill Skowron to hit into a fast 6–4–3 double play.

So the score was tied at 3–all going into the bottom of the sixth, when Frank Malzone led off with a base hit. That was when Casey Stengel went to his bench for a series of pinch hitters. Since Friend was a righty, Casey wanted some left-handed batters to face him. His first choice was Yogi Berra to bat for Triandos. The Baltimore fans didn't like that because Triandos played for the Orioles. They booed poor Yogi, who popped out.

Stengel then sent up Ted Williams to bat for shortstop Luis Aparicio. Ted sent a bouncer to third, but Frank

Thomas couldn't get the ball out of his glove. When he did, he dropped it. Both hands were safe.

Once more, Stengel sent up a pinch hitter, this time, Gil McDougald. Finally, Casey guessed right. Gil sent a looping fly to left center to score Malzone with the go-ahead run.

Billy O'Dell, one of Baltimore's crack pitchers, came in for the American League to start the seventh. Pinch hitter Johnny Logan teed off and sent a long drive to left. Ted Williams, who was a better fielder than most people thought, made a leaping catch to snare the liner. Logan was the last National League batter to come close to getting a hit off O'Dell. The next two batters went out via routine grounders. In the eighth, O'Dell set the National Leaguers down with two grounders and a strikeout. In the ninth, the best the batters could do was a pop foul, another strikeout, and a pop-up. O'Dell needed just twenty-seven pitches in three innings to go through nine batters. If there was a star player in the 1958 all-star game, it certainly was Billy O'Dell.

It had not been a particularly exciting game. Not one extra-base hit had been struck, and the 4–3 score was ordinary in that there were no spectacular rallies in the late innings. But it was a great game for other reasons. It was, after all, the game's silver anniversary. And it was Casey Stengel's third victory in all-star competition.

The win, however, worried Stengel a little. When he won his first all-star game in 1954, he lost the pennant that year to Cleveland. When he won the all-star game in 1957, he lost the World Series to Milwaukee. Now he had won again in 1958. What dreadful loss awaited him in the near future?

BOX SCORES

AMERICAN

	ab	r	h	rbi
Fox, Chi. 2b	4	1	2	1
Mantle, NY cf	2	0	1	0
Jensen, Bost. rf	4	0	0	1
Cerv, KC lf	2	0	1	0
O'Dell, Balt. p	0	0	0	0
Skowron, NY 1b	4	0	0	0
Malzone, Bost. 3b	4	1	1	0
Triandos, Balt. c	2	0	1	0
Berra, NY c	2	0	0	0
Aparicio, Chi. ss	2	1	0	0
Williams, Bost. lf	2	0	0	0
Kaline, Det. lf	0	0	0	0
Turley, NY p	0	0	0	0
Narleski, Cleve. p	1	0	1	0
Vernon, Cleve.	1	1	1	0
Wynn, Cleve. p	0	0	0	0
McDougald, NY ss	1	0	1	1
	31	4	9	3

NATIONAL

	ab	r	h	rbi
Mays, SF cf	4	2	1	0
Skinner, Pitt. lf	3	0	1	1
Walls, Chi. lf	1	0	0	0
Musial, St. L. 1b	4	1	1	0
Aaron, Mil. rf	2	0	0	1
Banks, Chi. ss	3	0	0	0
Thomas, Pitt. 3b	3	0	1	0
Mazeroski, Pitt. 2b	4	0	0	0
Crandall, Mil. c	4	0	0	0
Spahn, Mil. p	0	0	0	0
Blasingame, St. L.	1	0	0	0
Friend, Pitt. p	0	0	0	0
Jackson, St. L. p	0	0	0	0
Logan, Mil.	1	0	0	0
Farrell, Phil. p	0	0	0	0
	30	3	4	2

LINE SCORE

		R	H	E
National	210 000 000 =	3	4	2
American	110 011 00x =	4	9	2

Errors: Banks, Triandos, Fox, Thomas. Double plays (4). Left on base: American 7, National 5. Stolen base: Mays. Sacrifice: O'Dell. Bases on balls: off Turley 2, off Narleski 1, off Friend 2, off Farrell 1. Struck out: by O'Dell 2, by Farrell 4. Hits: off Spahn 5 in 3 innings; off Friend 4 in 2 1/3; off Jackson 0 in 2/3; off Farrell 0 in 2; off Turley 3 in 1 2/3; off Narleski 1 in 3 1/3; off Wynn 0 in 1; off O'Dell 0 in 3. Wild pitch: Turley. Hit by pitch: Turley. Winning pitcher—Wynn. Losing pitcher—Friend. Umpires: Rommel, Gorman, McKinley, Conlan, Umont, Secory.

July 7, 1959—
Forbes Field,
Pittsburgh

By 1959, the all-star game had become so popular with baseball fans that two games were scheduled. The first was played in Pittsburgh, the second in Los Angeles. Once again, the matchup of managers pitted Casey Stengel and Fred Haney against each other.

For Casey, 1958 had been a puzzling year. His American League team had won, which should have meant he had to lose either the pennant or the World Series. But he had won both. Was the jinx finally broken? Or, would the streak begin all over again with a loss in the all-star game?

1959 was a year in which neither Ted Williams nor Stan Musial was chosen by the players to make the starting team. But it was understandable. Both were having bad seasons, and both would finish out the year batting far under .300, for the first time in their major-league careers. But their respective managers selected them even if the players did not. What would an all-star game be without Williams and Musial?

Stengel and Haney seemed satisfied with their lineups.

The teams seemed evenly matched for a change. Each team had a total of 122 home runs. The heavy hitters in the American League squad included: Harmon Killebrew of the Washington Senators with 28; Rocky Colavito of Cleveland, who had 24; and Gus Triandos, the Baltimore catcher, with 20. The National League's leaders were: Eddie Mathews of Milwaukee, who had 25; Ernie Banks, with 23; and Hank Aaron, who had hit 22. Aaron was particularly fearsome. He was batting .370 with 72 runs batted in.

Haney started the Dodgers' Don Drysdale, a young right-hander. Drysdale pitched a good deal like Ewell Blackwell, delivering his fast ball with a sidearm motion. It was like a cross-fire to a right-handed batter. The ball would come by way of third base, and the batter naturally would step back, only to see the ball break across the plate for a strike. Ted Williams did not face Drysdale, but later, he jokingly said to the tall hurler, "Guys like you should be barred from baseball."

The American League failed to score on Drysdale during his three innings on the mound. The National League did score a run off Early Wynn on a homer by Eddie Mathews. Otherwise, it was a very quiet game so far.

After Wynn had finished his tour of duty, Stengel sent his prize relief pitcher, Ryne Duren, to take over. Duren was one of the most feared pitchers in the major leagues, partly because of his steaming fast ball, and also because of a little trick he and Yogi Berra had worked out. Duren, who was extremely nearsighted, wore glasses with lenses about as thick as the bottom of a Coke bottle. When he came in to relieve a Yankee starter, his first warm-up pitch would buzz in so high that it hit the base of the grandstand behind the plate.

"I guess Ryne's not feeling so good today," Yogi would confide to the batter. "You'd better not dig in at the plate. It looks like he doesn't have his control. The ball's liable to go anywhere. If he hits you, it'll be an accident."

The batters would watch Duren's blazer hum in high, or into the dirt, and decide it might be a good idea to get out of there as quickly as possible to avoid getting killed. Duren pitched three shutout innings, allowing just one hit and one walk. In the fourth inning, Al Kaline hit a home run off Lew Burdette to tie the score at 1–all.

When Jim Bunning took his turn after Duren, it seemed that the National League would do little damage for the rest of the game. The Detroit ace had been in twenty games for the Tigers, and his earned-run average was 0.90. That meant opposing teams had scored less than one run per game off him. Evidently, the National League didn't pay much attention to statistics. Ernie Banks clouted a two-bagger, and two outs later, Del Crandall singled him home. Crandall took second on the throw to the plate and scored the second run of the inning on Bill Mazeroski's single. The score was 3–1, with the National League ahead.

Elroy Face, Pittsburgh's crack reliever, was on the mound when the American League came to bat. Face's best pitch was a fork ball, delivered from between the middle and index fingers. When the fork ball was working properly, it would come straight in and then drop down abruptly. Opposing batters described the pitch as "a ball falling off a table."

However, Face did not have his stuff. With two out, Nellie Fox dunked a hit, Harvey Kuenn walked, and Kansas City's Vic Power singled in Fox. Ted Williams batted for Colavito and drew a pass to load the bases. Gus Trian-

Willie Mays, San Francisco Giants' slugger, comes into third in the eighth inning of the 1959 all-star game to score Hank Aaron and win the game for the National League, 5–4.

Ed Matthews, Milwaukee infielder, is congratulated by Hank Aaron at the plate, after blasting out the first homer of the 1959 all-star game for the National League.

dos came through with a line double down the left field foul line to chase home two more runs and put the American League in the lead, 4–3.

Whitey Ford, Stengel's marvelous southpaw, tried to protect the lead, but didn't do too well. Ken Boyer, of the Cardinals, singled, and Dick Groat sacrificed him to second. Hank Aaron smashed a hit to score Boyer and tie the game.

Then up came Willie Mays. In his heart, Stengel knew it was all over. Willie picked on Ford's fast ball and creamed a shot deep off the center-field wall, 436 feet from the plate, for the game-winning triple. The National League won, 5–4.

After the game, Ford sat in the locker room sadly shaking his head. "I have faced Willie Mays four times in all-star competition," he told reporters. "In 1955 in Milwaukee, Mays got two singles in two times at bat against me. In Washington, he hit a home run. Today he got a triple. I think Willie Mays owns me."

Casey Stengel was more philosophical. Because he had won the World Series in 1958, he felt that the old jinx would hold and that he would lose the 1959 all-star game. Besides, there was another game to play that year.

As it turned out, the American League won the second all-star game, 5–3. And the jinx worked. In 1959, the Yankees did not win the pennant, and Stengel did not manage the American League all-stars in 1960. That year, the Yankees won the pennant, but lost the World Series to the Pittsburgh Pirates. Stengel was fired by the Yankees because they claimed he was too old (he was seventy) to continue managing. He was replaced by Ralph Houk. Stengel was out of baseball temporarily, and he never managed the American all-stars again.

BOX SCORES

AMERICAN

	ab	r	h	rbi
Minoso, Cleve. lf	5	0	0	0
Fox, Chi. 2b	5	1	2	0
Kaline, Det. cf	3	1	1	1
Kuenn, Det. cf	1	1	0	0
Skowron, NY 1b	3	0	2	0
Power, KC 1b	1	1	1	1
Colavito, Cleve. rf	3	0	1	0
Williams, Bost.	0	0	0	0
McDougald, NY ss	0	0	0	0
Triandos, Balt. c	4	0	1	2
Mantle, NY rf	0	0	0	0
Killebrew, Wash. 3b	3	0	0	0
Bunning, Det. p	0	0	0	0
Runnels, Bost.	0	0	0	0
Sievers, Wash.	0	0	0	0
Ford, NY p	0	0	0	0
Daley, KC p	0	0	0	0
Aparicio, Chi. ss	3	0	0	0
Lollar, Chi. c	1	0	0	0
Wynn, Chi. p	1	0	0	0
Duren, NY p	1	0	0	0
Malzone, Bost. 2b	2	0	0	0
	36	4	8	4

NATIONAL

	ab	r	h	rbi
Temple, Cin. 2b	2	0	0	0
Musial, St. L.	1	0	0	0
Face, Pitt. p	0	0	0	0
Antonelli, SF p	0	0	0	0
Boyer, St. L. 3b	1	1	1	0
Mathews, Mil. 3b	1	1	1	1
Groat, Pitt.	0	0	0	0
Elston, Chi. p	0	0	0	0
Aaron, Mil. rf	4	1	2	1
Mays, SF cf	4	0	1	1
Banks, Chi. ss	3	1	2	0
Cepeda, SF 1b	4	0	0	0
Moon, LA lf	2	0	0	0
Crandall, Mil. c	3	1	1	1
Drysdale, LA p	1	0	0	0
Burdette, Mil. p	1	0	0	0
Mazeroski, Pitt. 2b	1	0	1	1
	28	5	9	5

LINE SCORE

				R	H	E
American	000	100	030 =	4	8	0
National	100	000	22x =	5	9	1

Error: Mathews. Two-base hits: Banks (2), Triandos. Three-base hit: Mays. Home runs: Mathews, Kaline. Sacrifice: Groat. Double plays (1). Left on base: American 8, National 4. Bases on balls: off Face 2, off Antonelli 1, off Wynn 1, off Duren 1. Struck out: by Drysdale 4, by Burdette 2, by Face 2, by Elston 1, by Wynn 3, by Duren 4, by Bunning 1, by Daley 1. Hits: off Drysdale 0 in 3 innings; off Burdette 4 in 3; off Face 3 in 1 2/3; off Duren 1 in 3; off Bunning 3 in 1; off Ford 3 in 1/3; off Daley 0 in 2/3. Wild pitch: Elston. Winning pitcher—Antonelli. Losing pitcher—Ford. Umpires: Barlick, Runge, Donatelli, Paparella, Crawford, Rice.

July 13, 1965— Bloomington, Minnesota

For Willie Mays, it was a treat to play in the 1965 all-star game. He would be coming home to visit his old fans.

In 1951, the Minneapolis Millers were a New York Giants farm team. Early in the season, the Giants were mired in fifth place in the National League. They needed help quickly. Leo Durocher had heard of a 20-year-old outfielder playing with the Millers, but he didn't know very much about him. Durocher put in a call to the Millers and spoke to Mays.

"What's your batting average?" Durocher asked. He was hoping that Mays was batting about .300 or more.

"I'm batting .477," Willie replied shyly.

"What!" Durocher could hardly believe his ears. "Could you hit about .250 in the big league?"

"I guess so," Mays said.

Minneapolis fans were stunned when Mays left the team. Horace Stoneham, owner of the Giants, took an ad in the Minneapolis newspapers, in which he apologized to the fans for "stealing away" their star center fielder. But surely they wanted to see their favorite player promoted to the big leagues, didn't they?

At first, Mays was a disappointment. He got no hits in his first twelve times at bat. In his thirteenth time at the plate, he hit a home run off Warren Spahn, the great Braves left-hander. But he did not get another hit in his next thirteen times at bat.

Mays was miserable and close to tears. He said to Leo Durocher, "Mr. Leo, I'm a failure. Maybe you should send me back to the Millers."

"That's stupid!" Durocher snapped. "You are my center fielder, Willie, from now on."

After the bad start, Mays righted himself. He hit only .274 in his rookie year, but twenty of his hits were home runs. As the years passed, he began to be compared with the great Joe DiMaggio as a fielder and batter. By 1965,

San Francisco Giants' outfielder, Willie Mays, hits the second pitch from the Orioles' Milt Pappas for a home run into the center field pavilion in the 1965 all-star game.

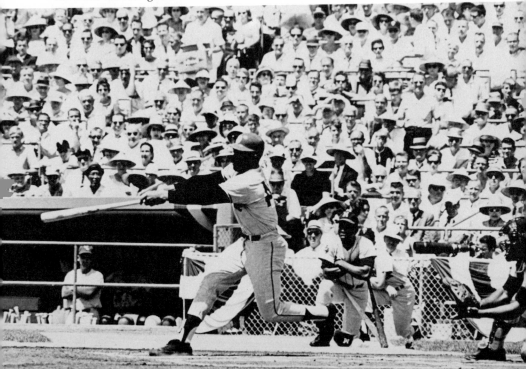

Mays was a full-fledged star, destined to be voted into the Hall of Fame.

As had happened once before, the managers of the 1965 all-star game were substitutes. Yogi Berra had managed the Yankees to victory in 1964, but he was fired after losing the World Series to the Cardinals. The Yanks then hired Cardinal manager Johnny Keane for their team. Berra couldn't manage the American League team because he was with the New York Mets of the National League. And Keane couldn't manage the National Leaguers because he was with the Yanks, an American League team. Their places were taken by Al Lopez of the White Sox and Gene Mauch of the Phillies.

Mays received a standing ovation as he stepped in as leadoff man to face Milt Pappas of the Baltimore Orioles. He swung at the first pitch and fouled it off. Then he took his cut at the next pitch and hammered it 400 feet into the left center field stands. It was his twenty-first hit in all-star competition, and it broke the record he had shared with Stan Musial.

Later, in the same inning, with a man on base, Joe Torre hit a long fly to left. The wind carried it farther and farther, until it hit the foul pole for another home run. The Nationals led, 3–0.

In the second inning, Willie Stargell, the strong boy of the Pittsburgh Pirates, hit a home run with one mate aboard. Now it was 5–0.

The American League seemed puny by comparison. Perhaps this was because the New York Yankees no longer had the great stars to bolster the all-star lineup. In the past, they had contributed such great players as Joe DiMaggio, King Kong Keller, Lefty Gomez, and Allie Reynolds. In

Chicago's third baseman Ron Santo crosses first base ahead of Minnesota's Zoilo Versailles' throw in the seventh inning of the 1965 all-star game.

the last few years, they also had Mickey Mantle and Whitey Ford. But both Mantle and Ford were now past the age of thirty-five. Mantle's legs were almost crippled from former injuries. Ford had lost his fast ball years before and was getting by on curves and off-speed pitches. To be sure, the American League still had a few sluggers, such as Harmon Killebrew of the Twins and Rocky Colavito of the Indians, but somehow it was not the same.

Now they were down by 5–0, and after two innings, the game seemed out of reach. The American League was being humiliated. When the all-star game started, the American League dominated the game, winning twelve of the first sixteen games. Then the National League began to catch up. Now, in 1965, the two leagues were tied with seventeen victories each, plus one tie game that had been called because of rain. But the American League refused to quit without a fight. They got one run in the fourth on Dick McAuliffe's single, a walk, a wild pitch, and Rocky Colavito's base hit. It wasn't an overpowering attack, but at least they were on the scoreboard.

One inning later, two swipes of the bat made it a tie game. McAuliffe homered with one on. Brooks Robinson legged out an infield hit, and Harmon Killebrew powered one into the left center stands.

The fates said that the National League had to win again. With runners on first and third, the Cubs' Ron Santo chopped a high bounder over the mound. Sam McDowell, the Cleveland hurler, leaped high but couldn't reach the ball. The runner on third broke for the plate and scored. It was only fitting that Willie Mays should score the winning run. It was 6–5, in favor of the Nationals. The American league continued to slump in the all-star game.

BOX SCORES

AMERICAN

	ab	r	h	rbi
McAuliffe, Det. ss	3	2	2	2
McDowell, Cleve. p	0	0	0	0
Oliva, Minn. rf	2	0	1	0
B. Robinson, Balt. 3b	4	1	1	0
Alvis, Cleve. 3b	1	0	0	0
Killebrew, Minn. 1b	3	1	1	2
Colavito, Cleve. rf	4	0	1	1
Fisher, Chi. p	0	0	0	0
Pepitone, NY	1	0	0	0
Horton, Det. lf	3	0	0	0
Mantilla, Bost. 2b	2	0	0	0
Richardson, NY 2b	2	0	0	0
Davalillo, Cleve. cf	2	0	1	0
Versalles, Minn. ss	1	0	0	0
Battey, Minn. c	2	0	0	0
Freehan, Det. c	1	0	1	0
Pappas, Balt. p	0	0	0	0
Grant, Minn. p	0	0	0	0
Kaline, Det.	1	0	0	0
Richert, Wash. p	0	0	0	0
Hall, Minn. cf	2	1	0	0
	34	5	8	5

NATIONAL

	ab	r	h	rbi
Mays, SF cf	3	2	1	1
Aaron, Mil. rf	5	0	1	0
Stargell, Pitt. lf	3	2	2	2
Clemente, Pitt. lf	2	0	0	0
Allen, Phil. 3b	3	0	1	0
Santo, Chi. 3b	2	0	1	1
Torre, Mil. c	4	1	1	2
Rose, Cin. 2b	2	0	0	0
Banks, Chi. 1b	4	0	2	0
Wills, LA ss	4	0	1	0
Cardenas, Phil. ss	0	0	0	0
Marichal, SF p	1	1	1	0
Rojas, Phil.	1	0	0	0
Maloney, Cin. p	0	0	0	0
Drysdale, LA p	0	0	0	0
F. Robinson, Cin.	1	0	0	0
Koufax, LA p	0	0	0	0
Farrell, Hous. p	0	0	0	0
Williams, Chi.	1	0	0	0
Gibson, St. L. p	0	0	0	0
	36	6	11	6

LINE SCORE

				R	H	E
National	320	000	100 =	6	11	0
American	000	140	000 =	5	8	0

Errors: None. Two-base hits: Oliva. Home runs: Mays, Torre, Stargell, McAuliffe, Killebrew. Sacrifice: Rose. Double plays (3). Left on base: National 7, American 8. Bases on balls: off Maloney 2, off Koufax 2, off Farrell 1, off Gibson 1, off Pappas 1, off Grant 1, off McDowell 1. Struck out: by Maloney 1, by Koufax 1, by Gibson 3, by Grant 3, by Richert 2, by McDowell 2. Hits: off Marichal 1 in 3 innings; Maloney 5 in 1 2/3; Drysdale 0 in 1/3; Koufax 0 in 1; Farrell 0 in 1; Gibson 2 in 2; Pappas 4 in 1; Grant 2 in 2; Richert 1 in 2; McDowell 3 in 2; Fisher 1 in 2. Winning pitcher–Koufax. Losing pitcher–McDowell. Umpires: Stevens, Meyer, Dimuro, Williams, Valentine, Kibler.

July 14, 1970—
Riverfront Stadium,
Cincinnati

In 1970, the fans chose the all-star teams for the first time since 1957. About two million ballots were collected by the Gillette Safety Razor Company, one of the television sponsors.

The players also named their choices, but they were unofficial. Mostly, the choices of the players agreed with those of the fans. Only at four positions did they differ. The fans chose Don Kessinger of the Cubs, a .281 batter, over Denis Menke of Houston, who was hitting .315. Willie Mays was selected with his .271 average over Roberto Clemente at .358. But the players also chose Willie McCovey, with his .259 average, over Dick Allen of St. Louis, who was batting .286. And they wanted Carl Yastrzemski at .301 over Tony Oliva at .328. So it could be said that the fans' choices were as good as those of the players.

A number of outstanding batters were not chosen. The National League could have started Billy Williams of the Cubs, who was batting .317, had 26 home runs, and 80 runs batted in. Or they could have selected the Reds' Bob Tolan, with his .323 average, 28 stolen bases, and 61 runs scored. As for Clemente, he threatened not to play at all. He said he would suddenly develop "a pain in the neck."

However, nothing could dampen the spirits of the 51,838 fans who jammed into the brand-new Riverfront Stadium.

Some veteran Cincinnati fans recalled a humorous incident that had happened at the old Crosley Field many years earlier. There had been a terrible flood when the Ohio River had overflowed into Mill Creek, and that little waterway backed up, too. When the nearby baseball field was completely under water, two Cincinnati players decided to have a little fun. They hired a rowboat and rowed over the center field fence while reporters looked on.

And there was another story the fans at the all-star game were buzzing about. It was the remarkable victory, the previous year, of the "Miracle New York Mets." The Mets were organized in time for the 1962 season, and they became a joke around the National League. It was a team of fumblers and bumblers, but the fans loved them. Casey Stengel came out of retirement to manage them, but he hung around only a couple of years. "The Ol' Perfessor" was too old for day-to-day baseball. But the Mets' management kept signing up good young players. They found Tom Seaver and Jerry Koosman, two marvelous young pitchers. They bought up Bud Harrelson, a slick-fielding, young shortstop. And they had Tommie Agee in center and Cleon Jones also in the outfield. Managed by Gil Hodges, the Mets went on to win the National League pennant, and then they defeated the Baltimore Orioles in the World Series.

"Amazin'," said Casey Stengel when he heard the news.

The final play of the 1970 all-star game gave the National League a 5–4 win. Above, Pete Rose starts for the plate, as catcher Ray Fosse waits for the throw; below, Rose slams into Fosse as he scores, while third-base coach Leo Durocher, rear, and Dick Dietz (2) watch.

Above, Rose slides across home; below, both players take a tumble.

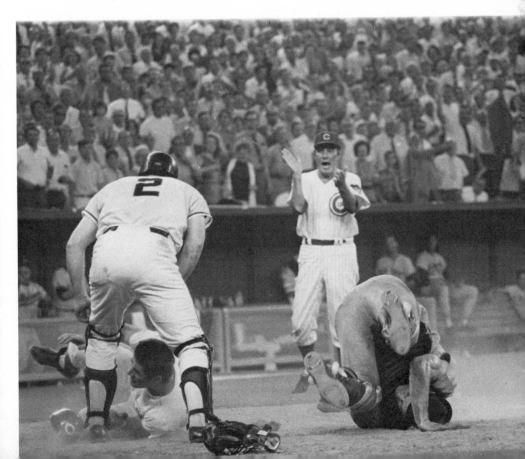

Each manager sent the ace of his staff to the mound to open the game. Earl Weaver relied on Jim Palmer of the Orioles, and Palmer came through handily. He allowed only one hit and fanned three. Tom Seaver of the Mets matched him pitch for pitch. He also permitted just one hit and struck out four.

The first run was tallied in the sixth inning by the American League. Catcher Ray Fosse got a hit off Gaylord Perry. He was sacrificed to second, and scored on a hit by Yastrzemski. They added another in the seventh with a pair of hits, a walk, and a sacrifice fly.

Jim Perry of the Twins, the older brother of Gaylord, was pitching for the American League when the Nationals broke the ice. They filled the bases with nobody out. Pinch hitter Willie McCovey smacked a grounder up the middle. Luis Aparicio, the Chicago White Sox shortstop, made a nice stop, tagged the runner coming from second, and pegged to first for the double play. The runner on third scored, but the rally was killed.

The American League added a couple of insurance runs on hits by Yaz and Willie Horton, plus a booming 400-foot triple by Brooks Robinson. The teams went into the last of the ninth with the American League leading, 4–1.

Two California players faced each other: Dick Dietz, the catcher of the San Francisco Giants, and Jim "Catfish" Hunter, the Oakland Athletics pitcher. Dietz got the better of the duel, with a long home run. Now the score was 4–2.

Bud Harrelson, the expert shortstop, continued the rally with a hit. One out later, Joe Morgan of the Houston Astros added another single. Then Earl Weaver made a pitching change. He brought in Fritz Peterson of the Yankees to face Willie McCovey. But the strategy didn't work. McCovey banged a hit to make the score 4–3.

Once more, Weaver changed pitchers. He brought in another Yankee, Mel Stottlemyre, to pitch to Roberto Clemente, who had decided to play after all. Clemente sent a long fly to center field, tying the score.

Neither team could score in the tenth or eleventh innings. There were two out in the bottom of the twelfth, when Pete Rose of Cincinnati came to the plate. Years before, the Yankees' Whitey Ford had watched Pete Rose

The American League's Carl Yastrzemski slides safely into second with a double, as the ball gets away from shortstop Bud Harrelson during the 1970 all-star game. Yastrzemski was named the game's most valuable player. Giving the safe sign is second-base ump Frank Secory.

play his all-out brand of baseball. Rose had hit an ordinary fly ball for an out, but he ran at top speed to first. When the fly was caught, Rose sprinted back to the dugout. Ford chuckled and said, "Hey, look at 'Charlie Hustle' over there." It was a nickname that stuck. Nobody in baseball ever hustled like Pete Rose.

Rose got a single off Clyde Wright. Another hit by Grabarkowitz of Los Angeles followed. Jim Hickman came to the plate and lashed a liner over second for a hit.

Out in center field, Amos Otis picked up the ball and unleashed a good throw to the plate. Catcher Ray Fosse was blocking the plate as he waited for the throw. Pete Rose came steaming down the line. There was a tremendous collision at the plate. Fosse was knocked over backward; Rose went tumbling over home. The run scored. Again, the National League had won, 5–4.

Fosse was out of the lineup for a few days after that, and Pete Rose was pretty sore, too. Oddly, Fosse had gone to dinner at Rose's home only the previous evening. It was the first time the two players had met. After the collision, Rose said, "I like Fosse, he's a nice guy and a good player. But when I'm on the field, the only friends I have are wearing the same uniform I'm wearing. It's the only way I know how to play baseball."

BOX SCORES

AMERICAN

	ab	r	h	rbi
Aparicio, Chi. ss	6	0	0	0
Yastrzemski, Bost. 1b	6	1	4	1
F. Robinson, Balt. lf	3	0	0	0
Horton, Det. lf	2	1	2	0
Powell, Balt. 1b	3	0	0	0
Otis, KC cf	3	0	0	0
Killebrew, Minn. 3b	2	0	1	0
Harper, Mil.	0	0	0	0
B. Robinson, Balt. 3b	3	1	2	2
Howard, Wash. lf	2	0	0	0
Oliva, Minn. rf	2	0	1	0
D. Johnson, Balt. 2b	5	0	1	0
Wright, Cal. p	0	0	0	0
Freehan, Det. c	1	0	0	0
Fosse, Cleve. c	2	1	1	1
Palmer, Balt. p	1	0	0	0
A. Johnson, Cal.	1	0	0	0
J. Perry, Minn. p	0	0	0	0
Fregosi, Cal.	1	0	0	0
Hunter, Oak. p	0	0	0	0
Peterson, NY p	0	0	0	0
Stottlemyre, NY p	0	0	0	0
Alomar, Cal. 2b	1	0	0	0
	44	4	12	4

NATIONAL

	ab	r	h	rbi
Mays, SF cf	3	0	0	0
G. Perry, SF p	0	0	0	0
McCovey, SF 1b	2	0	1	1
Osteen, LA p	0	0	0	0
Torre, St. L.	1	0	0	0
Allen, St. L. 1b	3	0	0	0
Gibson, St. L. p	0	0	0	0
Clemente, Pitt. rf	1	0	0	1
Aaron, Mil. rf	2	0	0	0
Rose, Cin. lf	3	1	1	0
Perez, Cin. 3b	3	0	0	0
Grabarkowitz, LA 3b	3	0	1	0
Carty, Atl. lf	1	0	0	0
Hickman, Chi. 1b	4	0	1	1
Bench, Cin. c	3	0	0	0
Dietz, SF c	2	1	1	1
Kessinger, Chi. ss	2	0	2	0
Harrelson, NY ss	3	2	2	0
Beckert, Chi. 2b	2	0	0	0
Gaston, SD. cf	2	0	0	0
Seaver, NY p	0	0	0	0
Staub, Mont'l.	1	0	0	0
Merritt, Cin. p	0	0	0	0
Menke, Houst.	0	0	0	0
Morgan, Houst. 2b	2	1	1	0
	43	5	10	4

LINE SCORE

						R	H	E
American	000	001	120	000	=	4	12	0
National	000	000	103	001	=	5	10	0

Errors: None. Two-base hits: Oliva, Yastrzemski. Three-base hit: B. Robinson. Home run: Dietz. Sacrifice: McDowell. Hit by pitcher: by McDowell (1). Bases on balls: off Palmer 1, off McDowell 3, off J. Perry 1, off G. Perry 1, off Gibson 1, off Osteen 1. Struck out: by Palmer 3, by McDowell 3, by J. Perry 3, by Stottlemyre 1, by Seaver 4, by Merritt 1, by Gibson 2. Hits: off Palmer 1 in 3 innings; off McDowell 1 in 3; off J. Perry 1 in 2; off Hunter 3 in 1/3; off Peterson 1 in 0; off Stottlemyre 0 in 1 2/3; off Wright 3 in 1 1/3; off Seaver 1 in 3; off Merritt 1 in 2; off G. Perry 4 in 2; off Gibson 3 in 2; off Osteen 3 in 3. Winning pitcher—Osteen. Losing pitcher—Wright. Umpires: Barlick, Rice, Secory, Haller, Dezelan, Goetz.

July 20, 1977—
Yankee Stadium,
New York

How popular had the all-star game become? Perhaps a few numbers could tell part of the story.

In 1977, more than twelve-and-one-half million fans voted for the starting lineups. They cast their ballots at ball parks around the country. The game was televised by the NBC network. Ten cameras were situated at various parts of Yankee Stadium, plus one more in a blimp cruising overhead. A viewer, sitting at home, could see every play and every pitch even better than someone sitting in a box seat. Why, then, did 56,683 rabid rooters jam their way into Yankee Stadium? Because there was no substitute for seeing their favorite players in the flesh.

Yet there was something uncomfortable in the air. It seemed that every good player in both leagues almost demanded to be chosen for the starting lineup. No, they did not quarrel too much with the choice of the fans. But, from time to time, there was a good deal of grumbling.

In 1970, Roberto Clemente said he might not play because the fans did not select him. But he had a change of heart and did get into the game. He drove in an important run with a long fly ball.

In 1973, the disgruntled player was Nolan Ryan, the fireball pitcher of the California Angels. That year at the all-star break, Ryan was in the midst of a terrific season, when he set a modern major-league record of 383 strikeouts. He would pitch two no-hit games and two one-hitters. Yet, Dick Williams, manager of the champion Oakland Athletics, had not picked him for the American League pitching staff. A great outcry was raised by the fans and sportswriters. In order to calm everybody, the commissioner himself had added one extra player to each team: Ryan to the American League and Willie Mays to the Nationals. But Ryan, who was still angry, vowed never to play in an all-star game again under such conditions.

In 1977, Billy Martin of the Yankees was the American League manager. Two of the pitchers he selected were Mark Fidrych of the Detroit Tigers and Frank Tanana of the California Angels. Once more, Nolan Ryan was overlooked, even though he sported a record of thirteen wins and only four losses, and more than 220 strikeouts.

A short time before the all-star game, Martin learned that both Fidrych and Tanana were out of action with arm injuries. Because the rules stated that at least one player from each team had to be on the squad, Martin chose Tiger first baseman Jason Thompson to replace Fidrych and Nolan Ryan to replace teammate Tanana. Ryan flatly refused to play.

"Why didn't he choose me in the beginning?" Ryan wanted to know.

Martin retorted that he used his own judgment, and that was the end of it. "Billy the Kid" Martin was a fiery

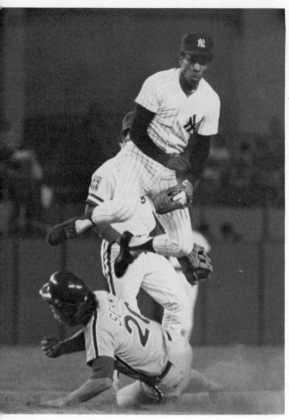

The New York Yankees' Willie Randolph, second baseman for the American League, throwing to first, after Mike Schmidt, of the Philadelphia Phillies, was forced out at second on a grounder by the Cincinnati Reds' Pete Rose in the 1977 all-star game.

leader, not accustomed to having his word questioned. He had only one thing on his mind—winning that all-star game.

The National League was on a winning streak. They had won six in a row, fourteen out of the last fifteen games. They were leading: the Nationals had won twenty-nine times, the American League eighteen, with one tie. Martin was going to try to overpower his rivals, and he had the sluggers to turn the tables. There were two heavy hitters from the Red Sox: George Scott with 25 home runs; and Jim Rice with 23. Larry Hisle had 21 and Graig Nettles had 20. That totaled 89 home runs for only four players.

Martin's pitchers weren't too bad either. He started

Jim Palmer, who seemed to win twenty games almost every season. Although Palmer did not look like a world beater then, the National League began to comb his deliveries as if he were throwing underhand.

Joe Morgan, now playing for Cincinnati, led off in the first inning and worked the count to three balls and two strikes. Then he pickled Palmer's next pitch into the right field stands for a round tripper. Steve Garvey struck out, but Pittsburgh's Dave Parker singled. George Foster sent him around with a long double. Greg Luzinski of the Phillies also ran the count to 3–and–2. Then he slammed one into the right field stands to make the score 4–0. In the third inning, Steve Garvey entered the home-run derby with his own clout deep to left. That made it 5–0.

Like many all-star games in the past, there was good fielding by both sides. In the third, George Foster almost climbed the wall to snare a long drive by Rod Carew, robbing the Minnesota star of a sure two-bagger. The American League infield did the job admirably, converting hard-hit grounders into outs.

But defense wasn't getting any runs on the board for the American League. Don Sutton of the Dodgers stopped them in their tracks. They finally broke through on a single by Carew, a walk to Fred Lynn, and a double by Richie Zisk that scored a pair. Later, they added another, when Garry Templeton of the Giants messed up a sure double-play ball. Willie Randolph of the Yanks cashed in the run with a base hit to make the score 5–3, in favor of the Nationals.

Sparky Lyle, the Yankee southpaw reliever, pitched the eighth. A double by Templeton atoned for his error. Lyle hit a batter and unfurled a wild pitch moving both

National League centerfielder George Foster, of the Cincinnati Reds, goes up against the outfield wall to catch a long ball off the bat of the Minnesota Twins' Rod Carew, of the American League, during the 1977 all-star game.

runners up a base. They scored on Dave Winfield's two-run single.

The American League showed some power in the bottom of the ninth. Bert Campaneris drew a free pass and George Scott finally reached the bleachers for two runs. But it was too little and too late. The National League did it again, 7–5.

The American Leaguers shuffled off the field, wondering what they had to do to beat their rivals in the other league. Both teams knew that, sooner or later, there would be another turn-around. In the beginning, the American League had almost run the Nationals off the field. Now they were being beaten. But there was always next year. There would always be an all-star game.

BOX SCORES

AMERICAN

	ab	r	h	rbi
Carew, Minn. 1b	3	1	1	0
Scott, Bost. 1b	2	1	1	2
Randolph, NY 2b	5	0	1	1
Brett, KC 3b	2	0	0	0
Campbell, Bost. p	0	0	0	0
Fairly, Tor.	1	0	0	0
Lyle, NY p	0	0	0	0
Munson, NY	1	0	0	0
Yastrzemski, Bost. cf	2	0	0	0
Lynn, Bost. cf	2	0	0	0
Zisk, Chi. lf	3	0	2	2
Singleton, Balt. rf	0	0	0	0
Jackson, NY rf	2	0	1	0
Rice, Bost. lf	2	0	1	0
Fisk, Bost. c	2	0	0	0
Wynegar, Minn. c	2	1	1	0
Burleson, Bost. ss	2	0	0	0
Campaneris, Tex. ss	1	1	0	0
Palmer, Balt. p	0	0	0	0
Kern, Cleve. p	0	0	0	0
Jones, Seatt.	1	0	0	0
Eckersley, Cleve. p	0	0	0	0
Hisle, Minn.	1	0	0	0
LaRoche, Cal. p	0	0	0	0
Nettles, NY 3b	2	0	0	0
	36	4	8	5

NATIONAL

	ab	r	h	rbi
Morgan, Cin. 2b	3	1	1	1
Trillo, Chi. 2b	2	0	0	0
Garvey, LA 1b	3	1	1	1
Montanez, Atl. 1b	2	0	0	0
Parker, Pitt. rf	3	1	1	0
Templeton, St. L. ss	1	1	1	0
Foster, Cin. cf	3	1	1	1
Morales, Pitt. cf	0	1	0	0
Luzinski, Phil. lf	2	1	1	2
Winfield, SD lf	2	0	2	2
Cey, LA 3b	2	0	0	0
Seaver, Cin. p	0	0	0	0
Smith, LA	1	0	1	0
Schmidt, Phil.	0	0	0	0
Reuschel, Chi. p	0	0	0	0
Sterns, NY c	0	0	0	0
Bench, Cin. c	2	0	0	0
Lavelle, SF p	0	0	0	0
Rose, Cin. 3b	2	0	0	0
Concepcion, Cin. ss	1	0	0	0
Valentine, Mont'l. rf	1	0	0	0
Sutton, LA p	0	0	0	0
Simmons, St. L. c	3	0	0	0
Gossage, Pitt. p	0	0	0	0
	33	7	9	7

LINE SCORE

					R	H	E
National	401	000	020	=	7	9	1
American	000	002	102	=	5	8	0

Error: Templeton. Two-base hits: Foster, Winfield, Zisk, Templeton. Home runs: Morgan, Luzinski, Garvey, Scott. Sacrifice: Sutton. Left on base: National 4, American 7. Double plays (2). Bases on balls: off Sutton 1, off Seaver 1, off Gossage 1, off Palmer 1, off LaRoche 1, off Campbell 1. Struck out: by Sutton 4, by Lavelle 2, by Seaver 2, by Gossage 2, by Palmer 3, by Kern 2, by Eckersley 1, by Campbell 2, by Lyle 1. Hits: off Sutton 1 in 3 innings; off Lavelle 1 in 2; off Seaver 4 in 2; off Reuschel 1 in 1; off Gossage 1 in 1; off Palmer 5 in 2; off Kern 0 in 1; off Eckersley 0 in 2; off LaRoche 1 in 1; off Campbell 0 in 1; off Lyle 3 in 2. Hit by pitcher: by Lyle (1), by Reuschel (1). Wild pitch: Palmer, Lyle. Winning pitcher—Sutton. Losing pitcher—Palmer. Umpires: Kunkel, Harvey, Phillips, Stello, Pulli, Brinkman.

Index

Campanella, Roy, 21, 25,
36
Campaneris, Bert, 82
Carew, Rod, 81
Carleton, Tex, x
Cerv, Bob, 55
Chandler, Spud, 16
Chapman, Ben, 5, 6
Chicago White Sox, ix
Clemente, Roberto, 70,
76, 78
Cleveland Indians, 40
Cobb, Ty, 52
Cochrane, Mickey, 8
Colavito, Rocky, 59, 60, 67
Comiskey Park, ix, 28
Consuegra, Sandy, 36, 38
Crandall, Del, 60
Cronin, Joe, 1, 4, 5, 8, 53
Cuyler, Kiki, 3, 6

Dickey, Bill, 1, 4, 5
Dietz, Dick, 74
DiMaggio, Dom, 12, 16,
24, 27
DiMaggio, Joe, 9, 10, 11,
12, 14, 15, 22, 23,
27, 34
Doby, Larry, 21, 31, 39
Dropo, Walt, 29
Drysdale, Don, 59
Duren, Ryne, 59, 60
Durocher, Leo, 64, 65

Ebbets Field, 21, 22
"The eephus ball," 17,
18, 19, 20

Face, Elroy, 60
Feller, Bob, 10, 11, 15, 18

Fenway Park, 10, 16
Ferriss, Dave "Boo," 16
Fidrych, Mark, 79
Foiles, Hank, 48
Forbes Field, 58
Ford, Whitey, 61, 62, 67
Fosse, Ray, 74, 76
Foster, George, 81
Fox, Nellie, 39, 47, 54,
55, 60
Foxx, Jimmy, x, 1, 3, 4, 5
Frick, Ford, 46
Friend, Bob, 55
Frisch, Frankie, ix, 1, 4,
5, 6

Garvey, Steve, 81
Gehrig, Lou, x, 1, 3, 4, 5
Gehringer, Charlie, x, 1, 3
Gomez, Lefty, 4, 5
Gordon, Joe, 14, 18
Gray, Ted, 31
Grim, Bob, 48
Grimm, Charlie, 38
Grimm, "Jolly Cholly,"
15
Groat, Dick, 61

Haney, Fred, 54, 58
Harrelson, Bud, 71, 74
Harris, Mickey, 16
Heath, Jeff, 11, 12
Heilmann, Harry, 52
Herman, Billy, 8
Hickman, Jim, 76
Hisle, Larry, 80
Hoak, Don, 46
Hodges, Gil, 25, 27, 48,
71

Hornsby, Rogers, 52
Horton, Willie, 74
Houk, Ralph, 62
Houtteman, Art, 34
Hubbell, Carl, x, 1, 3, 4
Hudson, Sid, 12
Hunter, Jim "Catfish," 74

Jablonski, Ray, 38
Jackson, "Shoeless" Joe, 52
Jansen, Larry, 31, 32
Jensen, Jackie, 54, 55
Jersey City Giants, 21
Jones, Cleon, 71
Jones, "Puddin'head," 31
Joost, Eddie, 27

Kaline, Al, 47, 48, 60
Kansas City Monarchs, 21
Kasak, Eddie, 24, 25
Keane, Johnny, 66.
Kell, George, 24, 27, 31, 45, 46
Keller, Charlie "King Kong," 6, 18
Keltner, Kenny, 14
Kessinger, Don, 70
Killebrew, Harmon, 59, 67
Kiner, Ralph, 25, 27, 28, 30, 31
Klein, Chuck, 6
Kluszewski, Ted, 38
Koosman, Jerry, 71
Kramer, Jack, 16, 18
Kuenn, Harvey, 44, 46, 60

Lajoie, Napoleon, 52
Lemon, Bob, 31

Lopez, Al, 8, 66
Luzinski, Greg, 81
Lyle, Sparky, 81
Lynn, Fred, 81

McAuliffe, Dick, 67
McCovey, Willie, 70, 74
McDougald, Gil, 45, 56
McDowell, Sam, 67
McGraw, John, 2
McKechnie, Bill, 14
McMillan, Roy, 46
Malzone, Frank, 45, 46, 48, 55, 56
Mantle, Mickey, 36, 39, 46, 50, 51, 54, 55, 67
Manush, Heinie, x, 1, 3
Martin, Billy, 79
Martin, "Pepper," 6
Mathews, Eddie, 48, 59
Mauch, Gene, 66
Mays, Willie, 46, 47, 48, 54, 61, 62, 64, 65, 66, 68, 70, 79
Mazeroski, Bill, 55, 60
Medwick, Joe "Ducky," 1, 3, 5
Memorial Stadium, 50
Menke, Dennis, 70
Michaels, Cass, 31
Miller, Eddie, 14
Milwaukee Braves, 56
Minneapolis Millers, 64
Minoso, Minnie, 36, 38, 48
Mize, Johnny, 12, 24
Morgan, Joe, 74, 81
Mossi, Don, 48
Mueller, Don, 38
Mungo, Van Lingle, 5